Women Against Tyranny:
Poems of Resistance during the Holocaust

For Alice
with best wishes
Dave Walden

I thought you
might find this manner
of presenting the history
of women interesting
Merry Christmas
Love,
Mom

Dedication

This book is dedicated to the memory of my parents, Meyer and Pearl Dubrow, and to Larry, Andrea, Andy, Natalie, Simeon, Noah, Lev, Owen, Aaron, and Caleb.

Also by Davi Walders

Poetry (Books and Chapbooks)

Using Poetry in Therapeutic Settings: A Resource Manual & Poetry Collection
Gifts: Poem Portraits of Gifted Individuals who Valued Giving
Afternoon in the Garden: Poems by Davi Walders

Other

Comfort Cards: American Hospice Foundation

"A little longer and the wicked is no more;
you will look at where he was—
he will be gone" (Psalm 37:10)

Psalm translations from the *JPS Hebrew-English Tanakh,* Jewish Publication Society, first pocket edition, Philadephia, PA, 2003.

Women Against Tyranny

Poems of Resistance during the Holocaust

Davi Walders

CLEMSON UNIVERSITY
DIGITAL PRESS

Works produced at Clemson University by the Center for Electronic and Digital Publishing, including *The South Carolina Review* and its themed series "Virginia Woolf International," "Ireland in the Arts and Humanities," and "James Dickey Revisited," may be found at our Web site: http://www.clemson.edu/caah/cedp. Contact the director at 864-656-5399 for information.

CLEMSON UNIVERSITY
DIGITAL PRESS

Published by Clemson University Digital Press at the Center for Electronic and Digital Publishing, Clemson University, Clemson, South Carolina.

Produced with the Adobe Creative Suite CS5 and Microsoft Word. This book is set in Adobe Garamond Pro and was printed by Standard Register.

Editorial Assistant: Emily Kudeviz.

Cover Design: Charis Chapman and Christina Cook

To order copies, contact the Center for Electronic and Digital Publishing, Strode Tower, Box 340522, Clemson University, Clemson, South Carolina 29634-0522. An order form is available at the digital press Web site (see above).

Table of Contents

&

PART ONE
Prologue

PART TWO
"Though War Rise Up Against Me"

PART THREE
Picture Gallery

Part Four
Epilogue

A Note on the Author

List of Illustrations

PICTURE GALLERY

Foreword

by Debra Leigh Scott
Hidden River Arts

It is always a joy when an artist takes on a subject that is large, powerful and important. Davi Walders does just that with *Women Against Tyranny: Poems of Resistance During the Holocaust.* Her work tells the important stories of the women, Christian, Muslim, and Jewish, who risked their own lives, working as resisters throughout Europe during one of the most terrifying times in human history. While much has been written about the horrors and heroes of that time, too little has been written about the women, who have been largely overlooked. Walders works to give voice to the silence surrounding these heroines, who ran dangerous underground operations, tracked enemy activity, administered to the sick, wounded and dying, protected and transported downed pilots and took children on dangerous trips across the Alps. Long ignored in World War II histories, these women deserve the attention, respect and honor Walders has worked to give them.

It has been a long labor of love for Davi, who has worked for fifteen years on this collection, searching for the forgotten or ignored stories of these women. She has traveled to Prague, Vienna, Norway, France, Denmark....anywhere the search for their stories took her.

In her own words, "The women include Dr. Rita Levi Montalcini, a Nobel Prize in Medicine recipient; Dr. Roza Papo, doctor and first female general in Tito's army; Emilie Schindler, Oskar Schindler's wife, who saved hundreds of people but was left out of the movie *Schindler's List*; and Magda Trocme, one of the leaders of Chambon-sur-Lignon, the French village which hid thousands of Jews and other refugees." These women, and others, were waiting for Davi, whose art would coax them out of the shadows.

The stories are told through Davi's poetry. Part of the book also recounts her own personal journey in search of the stories of these women. A woman searching for lost women, Davi herself enters history, moving backwards in time to rescue the rescuers, to hear the voice, envision the essence of each. She does nothing less than resurrect them, breathe life into their forgotten identities, and sing their stories.

As Founder of Hidden River Arts, I have run a residency program which offered time, solitude and support for artists in the midst of important projects. I can't imagine a more worthy project than this one, and it was exciting and gratifying to be able to offer Davi support when she needed it. I remember the day her proposal arrived. Looking through her materials, and reading her plans for this very ambitious project, I could feel her passion and determination. I could sense the urgency with which she was called to reclaim these women. That Hidden River has played any small part in offering some assistance to her journey and her endeavor gives me joy.

The years of her hard work and travels have paid handsomely. This is an important book. Through Davi's poetry, these women come into focus, take form and live again. Their histories, their passions, their bravery become real to us in a way that will never allow them to be silenced and forgotten again.

Preface

by Davi Walders

For as long as I can remember, I have been unusually aware of silence and absence—of whose voices and faces are present; whose are missing. The poem "Greenhorns" comes out of that sensitivity as does this book.

My father walked across war-torn Europe at a very young age with his mother after my grandfather, a fruit peddler who earned citizenship in Hartford, Connecticut, sent for them. My grandfather brought them out of the *shtetls* that would be decimated by the Nazis during World War II. My father refused to speak of that terrifying wandering, and I knew not to ask.

"Greenhorns" also arises from my appreciation of our immigrant family—the fact that their sacrifices gave me the gift of being born in the oil fields of west Texas during the War when many of our relatives were locked in the inferno of Europe. My father rode the rails to attend college on a scholarship at New Mexico School of Mines during the Depression. He rose to a position of leadership in a major oil company, the first Jew to do so. Outwardly his story is one of perseverance and success, but the trauma and displacement were buried deep within. Why didn't he speak of childhood? What stories were silenced?

These questions remained inchoate within me until coming into focus during travel in France as my husband and I drove through small villages in Burgundy, each with its monuments to its townspeople who resisted the Nazis. I read the names on the monuments. What was most striking were the absences—Where were women's names?

What began with my father's story and the memory of the monuments without names became an obsession to fill the silence. More than doing research, I became a rag picker hunting for remnants. I read. I applied for research grants. I read more. I took buses to Anne Masse, France; Stutthof, Poland; Lidice, Czech Republic. I scoured archives, wandered gravesites. I went wherever there might be stories of those who were missing or forgotten.

This work has been a long and difficult journey. Ten death camps in ten days traveling with the U.S. Holocaust Memorial Museum. Spending weeks alone in libraries and archives. Refraining from writing when sadness overwhelmed me. Fighting the depression that comes when dealing with cruelty and death. Then getting back to this work, because nothing compares to the journeys these women took to save others, themselves, and the world.

Over the years of working on this collection, I received unexpected gifts when I mentioned I was searching for stories of women's resistance. While at a conference on an entirely different subject in Minnesota, I happened to sit next to someone who knew Magda Trocme's daughter. who lived in St. Paul. Spending the day with Nelly Trocme Hewett, sitting at dinner across the table from a woman who told me I had to include Corrie Ten Boom, whom, until that moment, I knew nothing about; someone bringing me a poem written by Marianne Cohn, saying she understood that I would know what to do with it—among all these gifts were opportunities to work with survivors, to help them write their own stories, to listen to rescuers and those rescued by Jews, Christians, and Muslims. These serendipities often came at my lowest moments.

The search to find and give voice to these women's stories has guided me for fifteen years. I could not turn away from this enriching and ennobling work. So I hope you will be touched as I have been by these women's bravery and sacrifice.

GREENHORNS

He came to a bungalow near here, just down Zion
Street, at eight or nine or ten. Who was sure
in the *shtetl* where the future strangled between
starvation and conscription, where it was safer
without records. Only the year and month of his
arrival are certain, logged at Ellis Island along
with de-licing information. A new name, tailored
by a clerk who tossed circumcised syllables into
trash bins in the long hall. It was the year before
they shut the gates on types like him, like us,
and the uncle never to be seen again. His father
awaits him, the father he doesn't remember,
who packed into steerage, stacked in the stench
of others and sailed to the *goldeneh medinah*
seven years earlier. His father who found a nickel,
bought apples, made a dime, saved a nickel, bought
apples, and sent tiny sums month after month, until
he earned citizenship, a horse, a cart, passage
for a son, a wife, but not the twin whose name
burns with millions in the black books
above the flame. "Last seen: Sobibor, 1943,"
reads the last tome of D's at *Yad Vashem*.

Luck, pluck, timing, who knows, but your grandfather
made it, skinny from scarlet fever and a year
of silent walking at night, slipping cold rubles
into hands at borders and crossroads. A greenhorn,
a Jew, mute, mocked, overage, and overwhelmed
with joy in the first grade of the first school
he had ever been allowed to enter. How he must have
watched, listened and labored to learn, buy books,
a basketball, figuring it out letter by letter,
translating for parents who would never understand.
Little by little, game after game, he got it,
burying each piece of childhood in grades and letters,

xi

trading bullies for basketball, a scholarship, a world.
Erasing, becoming, erasing, becoming. Perhaps he talked
to someone. Perhaps he and his father sat one day
in the dusty yard of the rented bungalow just down
the street, peeled a perfect apple, tasted its sweet,
and he let it all pour out in Yiddish. More I cannot
tell you, except that he never ate tomatoes. "Poison,"
he mumbled. "Poison where I come from. Don't ask."
He never spoke of childhood. No pictures, no sitting
on his lap hearing his stories. Only ball, its pounding,
bouncing, baskets and points. 'Before basketball'
he locked into a silent fist that beat against the walls
of his heart until that muscle tired young, succumbed.

And so to you, this day, I say…may luck, pluck
and timing swing from your tassel, billow in your
robes as you march from the chapel across the green
to the waiting stage. And may you remember the gold
basketball that glints occasionally from your
jewelry box, the sweetness of plums and apples
sold not far from here, and the sweat and silence
of those who brought us here. And may you never know
the terrible price of such silence.

Acknowledgments

Grateful appreciation to so many whose generosity, knowledge, friendship, and assistance helped give birth to this book:

Molly Abramowitz, Mary Ellen Barrett (deceased), Perla Brandriss, Gordon Forbes, Carol Greenwald, Nelly Trocme Hewett, Diane Hovey, Susan Karchmer, Kathleen Kenyon, Wendy Kotler, Neil Kotler, Marcy Kraft, Gilah Landman, Debra Leigh Scott and the Hidden River Arts, Michel Margosis, Susan Massin, Johanna Neumann, Bett Notter, Joyce Press, Linda Raphael, Rabbi Marc Raphael, Gwenn Rosenthal, Ann Ratliff Russell, Rabbi Elchanan Sunny Schnitzer and members of Bethesda Jewish Congregation, Gail Schwartz, Coriolana Simon, Marguerite Striar (deceased), Robert Stumberg, Sundown Poetry Series of Piccolo Spoleto, Larry Walders, Marcia Frank Wasserstrom, Jane Winer, WIVLA of Houston, TX, Douglas Wolters.

PREVIOUS PUBLICATION ACKNOWLEDGMENTS

"In A Quiet Corner," "Marianne Baum: The Baum *Gruppe*," and "A Public Death, Still Chosen," appear in *Feminist Studies: Rethinking the Global*, Clair Moses, Editorial Director, Spring, 2010.

"Georgia O'Keeffe's *Yellow Cactus*" and "Only September," *South Carolina Review*, Clemson, SC Fall 2009.

"Under Verona's Trees," *Poetica* Magazine Website, August, 2009

"Greenhorns," *Bridges Journal*, Ann Arbor, MI, Spring 2009.

"Dr. Levi-Montalcini's Passion," *VPR* (*Valparaiso Poetry Review*) special re-publication, March, 2009.

"Wandering Sisters," accepted by *Lilith*, 2007, as yet unpublished.

"Stutthof, Sixty Years After," *International Feminist Journal of Politics*, vol. 9. Routledge, Taylor & Francis Group, Abingdon, Oxford, UK, Volume 9, 2007. Received the Marco Polo Award, Virginia Poetry Society, April, 2010.

"Blessed Is the Memory," *Midstream*, March/April, 2007

"Fighting With Nothing" and "Dr. Levi-Montalcini's Passion," *Valparaiso Review*, Winter, 2006.

"The Practice of Dr. Adelaide Hautval" and "Art and Spirit (*Ars Longa*)" appeared in *Jewish Currents*, January, 2006.

"Lidice Survivor" appeared as "Almost Nowhere: Lidice" in *Tales From Nowhere*, Don George, ed., Lonely Planet Publications, Melbourne, Australia, 2006. Also appeared in *Travelers' Tales: Prague*, David Farley and Jessie Sholl, eds., Traveler's Tales Inc, Palo Alto, CA, 2006.

"R. U.," "General Dr. Roza Papo Reports from the Front," "Emilie's List," and "One White Rose" appeared in *Bridges: A Jewish Feminist Journal Special Edition: Resistance Is*, Indiana University Press, 2006.

"*Zegota*" appeared in *Lilith*, Summer, 2005.

"Killing the Wagner-Rogers Bill," *Jewish Women's Literary Annual*, New York, NY, 2005.

"Heading East" appears in *Beyond Lament: Poets of The World Bearing Witness to the Holocaust*, Marguerite Striar, ed. Northwestern University Press, Evanston, IL, 1998.

"Monument Near Luzy" has been published numerous places including *Feminist Studies* and *Potomac Review*.

I AM GRATEFUL TO THE FOLLOWING

The Puffin Foundation for a 2007 grant to continue research on women's resistance and music from the World War II period and to develop a program interweaving music from the period with poetry of women's resistance.

Hidden River Arts Grant for research and writing support, 2006.

ECO Grant from Women in the Visual and Literary Arts (WIVLA), Houston, TX, 2005, to assist with research and revision.

A second Jenny McKean Moore Poetry Workshop Fellowship at George Washington University, 2005, where several of these poems were critiqued.

A second opportunity to read at the Sundown Series at Piccolo Spoleto, Charleston, SC, 2005, when several of these poems were first read before an audience.

Research and writing support provided by a Time Out Grant for Women from Cross Currents and the Luce Foundation, October, 2000, and February, 2001.

Sarah Crouch and other librarians at the U.S. Holocaust Memorial Museum.

I appreciate the early recognition of four small Holocaust poems which won first place in the 1995 Franklin Dew Award Competition sponsored by the Virginia Poetry Society.

I am grateful for the continuous support and assistance of the Washington, DC Ladies Roundtable.

I am grateful for the research and technical support of Molly Abramowitz at the United States Holocaust Memorial Museum.

I am grateful for the opportunity to talk and work with survivors, whose generosity and spirit astound me to this day.

Preview Notices

Davi Walders has written an important book that brings to light many of the roles women played in resistance to the Holocaust. This is history that is exciting and inspiring.

Marge Piercy
Author of *The Moon Is Always Female*, *The Art of Blessing the Day*, *Colors Passing Through Us*, and other collections of poetry
Cape Cod, Massachusetts

ॐ

This is a unique and extraordinary collection of poems and narratives which opens new avenues of representation for teaching Holocaust literature. Davi Walders knows so many Holocaust heroes (e.g. Dr. Rita Levi-Monatalcini, Sophie Scholl, Corrie Ten Boom, Zivia Lubetkin) so well that she writes persona poems, poems in the voices of the women themselves. I cannot imagine teaching Holocaust literature without "The Silence at Treblinka" or "Two Glimpses of History" or any of the invaluable texts she now offers teachers and readers who are willing to open themselves to new and even startling voices.

Marc Lee Raphael
Nathan and Sophia Gumenick Professor of Judaic Studies
The College of William and Mary

ॐ

With the publication of *Women Against Tyranny*, Davi Walders gives recognition to the women who fought for human rights, sacrificed their lives in many cases and in the process saved many innocent lives.

It is a most important task that Mrs. Walders has undertaken since giving due recognition to these courageous women has been long overdue.

I hope that many young people and future generations will read this book and will learn from it to what incredible acts of inhumanity men can stoop while others will give their lives in order to save men, women and children. Albania and its people are a great example.

Johanna Neuman
Silver Spring, Maryland
(rescued in Albania)

ॐ

Davi captures, in her work, the spirit of everyone who wanders the old country looking for their roots. This collection takes the reader to the courageous experiences of the generation before us.

Rabbi Elchanan Sunny Schnitzer
Bethesda Jewish Congregation
Bethesda, Maryland

ॐ

Davi Walders exhibits an ability to draw readers toward historical events or figures in a compelling manner that evokes powerful emotional and psychological reactions. The poetry focuses on close examination of details, objects, behavior, and atmosphere, inviting a more intimate view of human characteristics that reveal those devoted depths of spirit and energy necessary to make possible an individual's most passionate actions.

Edward Byrne
Valparaiso University

ॐ

You must understand. We had to do something. So speaks one of the courageous women who did what they could and what they knew they had to do during the *sho'a* and who come to life in Davi Walders's dedicated work. Walders, too, has done something necessary and important in giving voice to this silent part of our history.

Marcia Falk
Author of *The Book of Blessings* and *The Song of Songs: Love Lyrics from the Bible*

PART ONE
Prologue

"For I have heard the whispering
of man, terror on every side"
(Psalm 31:14)

KILLING THE WAGNER-ROGERS BILL

There are so many ways to let things die:
committee recesses, members taken ill,
called away moments before a vote, closed-
door actions or just not showing up.

Most things don't even require
a filibuster. There are quieter ways—
argue wording, delete, tack on, amend
the bill to death so that even sponsors

can't stomach the language they wrought.
They tried, oh, they tried, Mr. Wagner
and Mrs. Rogers, the senior Dingell, too,
that spring and summer of 1940,

but the Capitol was hot and sweating
with America-Firsters and superpatriots
who did not want those children, not
those odd children, not children with

dark hair and dark eyes, not those Jewish
children from Germany. Later, children
from Britain would be all right, a country's
duty even, but not yet, not for those

twenty thousand children with terrified
eyes, whose parents had already disappeared,
not that summer when it was so hot that
things just died quietly behind closed doors.

GEORGIA O'KEEFFE PAINTING *YELLOW CACTUS*

A woman sits painting in the desert. She perches
on a rickety chair beside her old Ford. She has said

she doesn't like flowers much, prefers cactus, rock,
and bone, but here she is again, daubing, cutting,

cropping, closing in on the flowers of a prickly pear
she has studied all morning before crowning it

with rough brush and bright yellow, taming it gold
above thorns. A painter sits drinking in the silent heat,

drenching a canvas with pale greens and bits
of bursting yellow while the world is blowing up.

Country after country falls to bombs and goosesteps,
Dunkirk empties, the Blitz shrieks terror into shelters

and they strut into Paris, looting museums and homes
because they so love art, rounding up artists and poets

because they so detest degenerates while, here, a painter
sits in the desert that desperate spring of 1940 feeling

her way between bristles and blossoms, magnifying
between spines, a small, safe world in bright, full bloom.

Yellow Cactus (12x16 inches, painted in 1940) is owned by the Maier Museum of Art of Randolph-
Macon Woman's College in Lynchburg, VA.

Monument Near Luzy

Dark and close, the lower path sweats
like a bog after rain. Finches slip
between verbena and new green pine.
There is no marker. Only *camp* and
a dim arrow on a splintered gate
point to the higher plateau. A grove

of trees almost hides it. Mortar crumbles
into the damp hole, once a bunker.
Mossy beams cast shadows where earth
has fallen in. On clear nights, the women
parachuted here or slipped silent from
flimsy Lysanders,[1] spreading north and south

like foxes gone to ground. Along *ligne*[2]
after *ligne*—Odile, Francoise, Marie Claire—
they carried messages, money, and explosives,
returned with downed fliers, exhausted
escapees. Liaison women exposed on all
sides, here they radioed and rested before

betrayals dragged them to Ravensbruck,
Dachau, Auschwitz where even into dark
dawns of 1945, they were carried,
helped to stand and turned just so,
so that one small bullet could
penetrate the exact spot in the back

of the neck. Luzy, Onlay, St. Honore
Les Bains, small towns near Vichy, small
cells of resistance, women moving in
and out of darkness, light and flame.
The monument at roadside: *Ruines du Camp
Maquis Louis.* Names chiseled in marble:

---

1. Lysanders: very light planes used to transport parachutists into France.
2. *lignes*: covert networks taking people out of France.

petits fonctionnaires, mayors, farmers,
pharmacists. Only the women have disappeared:
Violette Szabo, Denise Bloch, Lillian Rolphe,
Mother Maria, Sister Marie-Laurence, mothers
and daughters like the Dumons and de Greefs.
Odette Churchill, Genevieve DeGaulle,

Countesses Milleville and Panouse, *garagistes*,[3]
waitresses and widows who pedaled along
the side of the road bearing gifts
of intelligence like stilletos behind
bright smiles. Born in those moments
of that war, I can only gather their names,

a brush, some paint, a pen, some ink.
Yellow paint, black ink, thick lest
the markers splinter and dim. Small towns,
small cells, women whirled into that awful,
other dancing. The silence is dark
and close here. Where are their names?

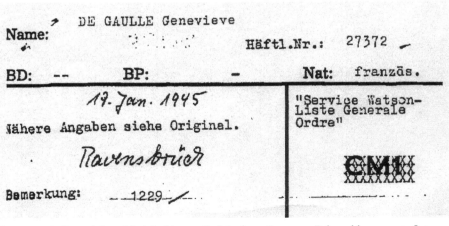

Document 1: Record from Nazi Archives at Bad Arolsen, Germany. Released by treaty to International Tracing Service and the U.S. Holocaust Memorial Museum, 2008

---

3.   garagistes: female mechanics.

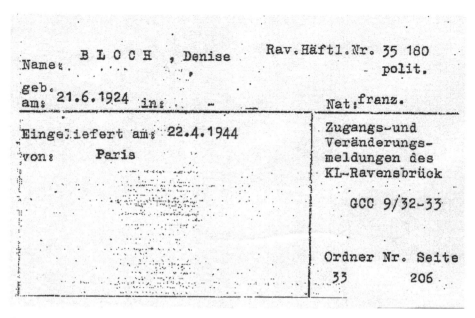

Name:	B L O C H , Denise	Rav.Häftl.Nr. 35 180

geb.
am: 21.6.1924 in:

Eingeliefert am: 22.4.1944
von: Paris

Rav.Häftl.Nr. 35 180
- polit.

Nat:franz.

Zugangs-und
Veränderungs-
meldungen des
KL-Ravensbrück

GCC 9/32-33

Ordner Nr. Seite
33   206

Document 2: Record from Nazi Archives at Bad Arolsen, Germany. Released by treaty to International Tracing Service and the U.S. Holocaust Memorial Museum, 2008.

Monument: A stele a few miles north of Luzy, France, marks the site of a base used by the Maquis Louis resistance group. A sign directs visitors to the nearby Musée de la Resistance de St. Honoré de Bains.

PART TWO

"Though war rise up against me"
(Psalm 27:3)

Marianne Baum (1913–March 4, 1943): German co-creator (with her husband) of the Baum Group (Baum *Gruppe*), a highly organized resistance group actively opposing the Nazis from 1937 until 1942 when most were arrested, tortured, sent to concentration camps or murdered by Nazis as was M. Baum.

CR

MARIANNE BAUM: THE BAUM *GRUPPE*

Act, do something, we told ourselves
and each other. And so we did—
our small group infiltrated factories,
organized slave laborers, wrote
pamphlets, dropped them on buses,
slipped out at night with buckets
of paint, brushes, left our mark.
So little, but we had to do something.

Then the anti-Soviet exhibit.
Goebbels' silliness to distract
from war losses, food shortages,
the freezing winter. It was not
difficult. We went, set explosives
here and there at the Lustgarten.
A match. Up it went. For a night,
flames danced with our resistance.
So little, but we had to do something.

They hunted us. Retaliation everywhere.
Then the *Sondergericht*—'special court.'
They carried me there, my shattered legs
dangling. No one talked. A hundred
Berliners rounded up for each of us.
Five hundred—most shot there and then;
the rest, slower deaths at Sachsenhausen.
This, too, our burden, but...would they
have died anyway? You must understand.

We had to do something.

Name: B A U M, Marianne

Geb.   Geb.
Dat.: 10.8.1910   Ort: Offenbach/Glan   Nat.:

Letzter Wohnort: Bad Münster a. Stein,   Rheinl. Pfalz
                 Hauptstrasse 39

Evakuiert: [ ]   Verzogen: [x]   Reg.Bez.:
                                                Koblenz
Ausgewandert: [ ]   Verstorben: [ ]

am: 1.10.1938

nach: Pirmasens, Hoefelsgasse 6   KK/LK:
                                                Kreuznach
in:

Bemerkung: Abmeldung:
1.12.38 = Kreuznach, Dessauerstr. 23

Document 3: Record from Nazi Archives at Bad Arolsen, Germany. Released by treaty to International Tracing Service and U.S. Holocaust Memorial Museum, 2008.

Friedl Dicker-Brandeis (1899–1944): Famous Czechoslovak artist who continuously taught art to the children imprisoned in Terezin from 1942 until she was deported and murdered at Auschwitz.

CR

ARS LONGA…

'FRIEDL DICKER-BRANDEIS EXCELLED PERMANENTLY,'
WALTER GROPIUS.

Friedl Dicker-Brandeis painted
little during the Terezin years—
starving, too crowded to think,
teaching the children every day.
Only an occasional work of her own.
"Flowers in a glass of water"
—a birthday gift smuggled in by
her students—fragile petals, pink
with life. *"Girl's Face"*—a hint
of cheekbones and hair, just
enough to frame a child's deep
blue eyes staring beyond walls.

You must look for her in her students'
work. Trace this tiny woman,
barely taller than her children,
in the five thousand pictures hidden,
left behind. See strokes of her
encouragement in Helena's collage:
Nazi-stained paper shredded into
frozen mountains and six-pointed
stars against an ink-black sky.
And in little Hanus' *"The Sea"*:
blue scraps arc into waves, his tiny
boat tossed in deep, opaque water.
Each creation carrying a child's
name and dreams in moments
between digging graves, hauling
corpses, emptying ashes into the river.

Friedl Dicker-Brandeis, holding
back the night with bits of charcoal,
smuggled paints, stolen paper

Bending over her students
in the cramped car, holding
a child in each hand between
dogs and guns as they were shoved
into the long Auschwitz tunnel
where they rose together
as October sparks, a teacher
and her children, their hidden
wisps of hope, buried behind.

Document 4: Record from Nazi Archives at Bad Arolsen, Germany. Released by treaty to International Tracing Service and U.S. Holocaust Memoria Museum, 2008.

Muriel Gardiner Buttinger (1901–1985)*:* An American heiress and medical student in Vienna who is thought to be the woman, Julia, described in Lillian Hellman's *Pentimento*. After WW II, Dr. Buttinger became a leading psychoanalyst in New Jersey.

CR

Muriel Gardiner Buttinger: an American in Austria

An inheritance from childhood teaches much:
always keep cash on hand, be generous, prepared.
Particularly in Vienna, particularly after the *Anschluss*,

particularly surrounded by fascism as she waited
for the money mailman, the *geldgrieftrager*, to bring
money from an account in Holland that would save lives.

These were her days in Vienna—studying medicine,
being analyzed by a Freud disciple, pretending to be
just an American student while noticing two anatomy

sections—one for Jews and Socialists, one for "real
Viennese"; noticing Jews deprived of graduation;
suddenly disappearing. Busy days, busy nights. Submitting

affidavits promising support for those desperate to leave,
procuring fake passports, taping them to her body under
a corset, moving back and forth from Vienna by night train

to Prague, walking mountain roads at night into Switzerland
to deliver passports, papers, and letters, even loaning her own
passport to any soul who looked a bit like her. Clandestine

meetings in the crowded heart clinic. Asking the code question,
'Are you waiting for Dr. Schwarz?' waiting to hear in return,
'Yes, but one always has to wait a long time,' slipping

fresh, precious passports into her shopping bag. Traveling
with those whose fake passport might give trouble. Always
ready to make a fuss if there were a search. Packing others'

jewelry in her own jewel case, carrying encrypted messages.
And still studying, taking exams, getting her medical degree
before taking the *SS Manhattan*, the last American ship out

of France home. Welcoming refugees into her apartment
in New York City, getting the sick ones free medical care,
going back to Europe as supervisor of the IRC[1] to help survivors

the minute the war ended. Still feeling she did not do enough.
If only others had done half what she did. If only others
had done a third what she did. If only...if only.

---

1.   IRC: International Rescue Committee.

Marianne Cohn (1922–1944)*:* French resister who led hundreds of children over the Alps to safety in Switzerland before being arrested and tortured to death by the Nazis three weeks before the liberation of Annemasse near the Swiss border in 1944.

Ↄ

A Late *Kaddish* for Marianne Cohn

'Not today will I betray....' from 'Je trahirai demain,'
the poem found in Marianne Cohn's pocket,
France, 1944.

I. The border

It is easy now. Train, bus, or tram.
Twenty minutes maximum from Annemasse
to Geneva, France to Switzerland.
In those years, as far away
as a dream of the Promised Land.
Today guards smile, joke,
and smoke. Borders are fluid
in towns of Haute Savoie, once
occupied by Italians, Vichy,
then the Nazis. Bound close
by the Jura, the Saleve, peaks
flattened by erosion and the Arve.
Plane trees barely move in July
heat. Above Annemasse, clouds
and hang gliders float slowly.
Carrefours.[1] Crossroads of Europe.
For her, it almost was.

---

1.   *carrefour*: crossroad.

II. *The plaques*

 1. *Hôtel du Pax.*

The early losses. Her country
first. Born Mannheim, 1922.
Hitler. Childhood interrupted.
Forever. Fleeing to Spain.
Civil War. Flight from Franco.
Another exile—seeking safety
in France. Her family—the first
round-up of foreigners. Imprisoned.
Gurs, then Drancy, then deported.
Among the early unlucky. UnFrench.
Undesirable. Unsafe. Marianne,
not twenty, escaping to the Jewish
underground. Transporting more
than two hundred children to safety
outside of France. "*Femmes
dans la nuit,*" they were called,
"night women." Young, brave,
determined. Another descriptor—
"*femmes fichues*"—done for.

The main street as it curves
toward the station just beyond
the square. Hot, dirty stone
walls. Requisitioned by Vichy,
turned into a prison by the Milice,
later the Gestapo. A bitter hole
of darkness and death. Records.
Fifteen hundred names neatly
listed in the register, some
underlined in red. "Mlle Cohn"
carries a red slash. How many
died here is not known. Only
how few were liberated.

The hotel again has its two
stars, 44 rooms. With breakfast,
300 francs. Geraniums droop
over balconies. Lace wilts
in windows. On the smoky wall
still pockmarked by bullet holes,
the shiny plaque. Small, gold

on black. "*Hommage d'Annemasse
à ces martyrs.*" A town honoring
its martyrs. Marianne Cohn,
"martyr," engraved in gold, just
above "*Français, souvenez-vous.*"[2]

2. *Monument du Charnier.*

Up higher, nearer the border.
Half an hour on foot.
It could have happened anywhere.
It happened here, in a small
grove behind the cemetery.
A cellmate said they came again
at midnight. Mlle Cohn borrowed
a toothbrush, a sanitary pad,
whispered words of Gandhi,
thought they would take her
to Montluc prison, to Barbie.
After four long years,
so much lost, so much learned,
she thought she might survive
even with torture. "*Une femme fichue.*"

August 23, 1944, five days after
the Annemasse liberation, six
bodies found in a shallow grave,
hastily dug. Hers, beaten
beyond recognition. Identified
only by her height, petite
as some of her children, and
her shoes. Bright eyes, kind
smile—gone. Just small shoes
on a bruised, broken body.
Tortured to death, dead before
the bullet. She divulged nothing.

---

2.   *souvenez-vous, souviens-toi:* remember

The forest is gone now. Just
the small grove, houses
and swingsets all around,
a clinic across the street.
Thin trees shade the monument
and a few marigolds needing
water. Plain marble, sitting
on bricks. 1944 and the names
are raised. Marianne Cohn,
the first of six. "*Lâchement
assassinés*," "cowardly murdered,"
chiseled on the stone. Further,
a plaque beneath the trees.
"*Charnier*"—monument of bones.
"*Français, souvenez-vous.*"

   3. L'École Primaire Marianne Cohn.

Wandering town streets, asking
for directions. People shrug.
No one recognizes her name.
Perhaps there, someone points
to a building beyond the park.
Rue Basten at Avenue Pasteur,
the old city-block of a school,
renamed in 1984, a generation
later when one of her saved
children returned, requested
Mlle Cohn be remembered.

Her last mission. July, 1944.
One month to liberation.
Four hundred meters from
the border. Arrested. Chained
with the children at *Hôtel du Pax*.
The resistance planned an escape.
Tuberculosis, sudden and contagious,
knowing the Nazi terror of disease.
They would call the town doctor,
a *résistant*. Frightened guards,
confusion. Such a raid had worked
elsewhere. But she refused.
Too risky with the children.

The Gestapo questioned
and threatened. She did not
break. Midnight, July 8,
she disappeared. Suddenly
there was no choice. The raid
to save the children. All of them
crowded in a covered truck,
crossing into Switzerland.
Now grandparents, they call it
a miracle—Mlle Cohn's miracle,
watching over them to see
that the *Pax* was not their tomb.

The school is empty. A tall fence
traps paper on concrete. July noon,
more than a half-century later. Silence
except for scraping leaves and motorcycles
backfiring in the distance. A sheet
taped to the door, reminding all
to return in September. The plaque
high on a pillar, her name dusty,
almost lost on grey granite.
The command in the familiar,
speaking to the school's children:
Marianne Cohn, killed for saving
32 children. "*Souviens-toi.*"

4. *Yad Vashem*

Who? They think they know. Like
the saved children, the murderers
slipped through Switzerland, then
home to live on with so many others,
protected after cooperating a bit
with Allied questioners. Nazis,
Gestapo, Vichy, *Milice*,[3] murderers.
Beyond grim days and nights
and years, beyond banal. Blue-black
and personal, an acrid gash.
Murderers. They have no other name.

---

3.   *milice*: Deadly, Nazi-supported French paramilitary force in Vichy, France.

Her children, spread throughout
the world, remember daily, visit
often the garden at *Yad Vashem*
where her name glistens on a small
plaque above pink-tipped roses
planted by their children.
They do not return to Annemasse
with its plaques, gold on black,
granite on marble. "*Français,
souvenez-vous.*" Some will see,
some will wonder, some will remember.

III. Her poem

> *Je trahirai demain*
>
> *Je trahirai demain pas aujourd'hui*
> *Aujourd'hui, arrachez-moi les ongles,*
> *Je ne trahirai pas.*
>
> *Vous ne savez pas le bout de mon courage.*
> *Moi je sais.*
> *Vous êtes cinq mains dures avec des bagues*
> *Vous avez aux pieds des chaussures*
> *Avec des clous.*
>
> *Je trahirai demain, pas aujourd'hui,*
> *Demain.*
> *Il me faut la nuit pour me résoudre,*
> *Il ne me faut pas moins d'une nuit*
> *Pour renier, pour abjurer, pour trahir.*
>
> *Pour renier mes amis,*
> *Pour abjurer le pain et le vin,*
> *Pour trahir la vie,*
> *Pour mourir.*
>
> *Je trahirai demain, pas aujourd'hui.*
> *La lime est sous le carreau,*
> *La lime n'est pas pour le barreau,*
> *La lime n'est pas pour le bourreau,*
> *La lime est pour mon poignet.*
>
> *Aujourd'hui je n'ai rien à dire,*
> *Je trahirai demain.*

[Je trahirai demain]
(translation)

> Tomorrow I will betray, not today
> Tear out my nails today. I will not betray.
> You don't know how long I can hold out,
> But I know.
>
> You are five rough hands with rings—
> You have hob-nailed boots on your feet.
> Tomorrow I will betray, not today.
> Tomorrow.
>
> I need the night to decide,
> I need at least one night, to renounce, to abjure, to betray.
> To betray my friends, to foreswear bread and wine,
> To betray life.
> To die.
> Tomorrow I will betray, not today.
>
> The file is under the floor,
> The file not for the window bars,
> The file not for the torturer,
> The file for my wrist.
>
> Today I have nothing to say,
> Tomorrow, I will betray.

Marianne Cohn, 1944

IV. *Souvenez-vous*

Someone gave me a copy of her
poem, found somewhere. No one
remembers exactly where.
The poem she scratched out
in dark nights, tucked in a pocket
the murderers didn't bother
to search. Found by the liberators
who wrapped and sat with her body,
unfolded the words, read silently
and aloud, over and over
in the charnel grove and wept.

I, too, received it, read it,
held it, taped it to my door,
reading as I enter, again
upon leaving until echo knit
silent into bone. "*Souvenez-vous,*"
the plaques say. I began to follow
the command. Her words walk with me,
rise in the dust of shoes stacked
in museums, rustle at long tables
in libraries, whisper in synagogues
and streets. Slivers that pierce,
cinders born on wind and air.
I wander and search. My door
stands ajar. Her poem waits there.

V. *A Late Kaddish*

Madness, perhaps, more than fifty
years after, to want to know
the whole of it, to wish they had
sent you somewhere, even Ravensbruck
those last days, where you might
have heard another's curse, where
even with torture, you might have
been comforted by Violette Szabo's
tapping, captured in the broken
mirror of Violette Rougier-Lecoq's
sketches, adopted by Lise Lesevre?
Somehow hung on.

What were they afraid of? Jews?
Women? Women Jews? Young women
Jews? Young women Jews saving
children? Or just Jews? Your murder,
just one more, was it a shovel
against bone or gun butts
against soft tissue? How many
participated? Holding? Striking?
Watching? It matters. I agree
with them. Records are important.

Yet I want more than facts.
Wrinkled cheeks, laugh lines,
angel hair crowning a high
forehead, defiant eyes, an old
woman, thin in blue or plump
in beige, surrounded by children
whose offspring close the circle.
I want many men to have pleased
you, your own children to have slid
from your womb onto playgrounds,
into graduation and wedding gowns.
I want more than plaques. I want
a woman still making poems—
poems free from a pocket, free
from my door. I want an old Jewish
woman singing, saving the world.

Gisi Fleischmann (1894–October 18, 1944): Leader of the Slovakian resistance who negotiated with Nazi leaders to ransom thousands of Jews. In March, 1943, she informed Zionist organizations in Geneva of the Lublin and Auschwitz exterminations. Arrested in 1944, deported in cattle car marked "R.U." and murdered at Auschwitz.

CR

'*R.U.*'[1]

Strange to sit alone, the entire car
emptied, marked '*R.U.*' only for me.
So odd to wait in silence after
all the ticking moments, hours,
years of constant begging, bartering,
pleading—anything for a life.
We did raise enough to stop
the deportations for a few months.
With Eichmann, Himmler, money whispers.
One must remember small successes.

The train has stopped; the beatings
will begin again. They cannot
believe I know nothing. We never
know, we must not know about others.
We are not that strong. I know only
this—each ransomed soul has moved
on—out of Poland, Bohemia, down
the Danube, across Slovakia, Hungary,
to the world of normal sorrows.

---

1.   *Ruckkehr Unerwunshch* (Return Not Desired) Sign on cattle car transporting Gisi Fleischmann to Auschwitz.

And why didn't I? After all
the others? My Paraguayan passport,
still hidden. I could not. I say
to my daughters in Palestine: "Love
each other. Live your lives."
For me, this measured ticking
ends, like the hours families
waited to be traded for trucks,
cloth, money. Goods for lives—
each one a precious remnant.
I step from the last train
into a silence just beginning.

Dr. Adelaide Hautval (1906–1988): French Protestant arrested in 1942 trying to get to her mother's funeral. She was imprisoned in Auschwitz and Ravensbruck until 1945. Her testimony was crucial in sentencing Nazi war criminals.

☙

THE PRACTICE OF DR. ADELAIDE HAUTVAL

Try to imagine her

a Gentile among Jews
a doctor among the sick
a prisoner rounded up

while trying to get home
for her mother's funeral,
an accidental arrest

plunging her into the cold
eye of evil, protesting
every step of the way

Bourges prison
arguing with the guards,
cursing each cruelty,

the cattle car
stitching "Friend of the Jews"
on her coat,

the Birkenau barracks
nursing the sick, hiding
those dying from typhus

Block 10
refusing to practice
Nazi 'gynecology'—refusing
to inject, irradiate,
sterilize, maim, disfigure—

Try to imagine her
surviving Auschwitz and Ravensbruck
to testify
that it was possible
to behave humanely

Try to imagine her—
Adelaide Hautval—a doctor
with a practice
in refusal.

Dr. med. HAUTVAL, Adelaide   *1724581*

1.1.1906 Hohbald/Niederrhein

War im KL Auschwitz

Hessisches Landeskriminalamt, Wiesbaden
7.1.81
                        15.1.81 Br.

                                        Häftl.Nr.:

Name: *Dr. HAUTVAL Adelaide*

geb.
am: in:

Weitere Angaben   Sachdok.-Ordner: *17*
siehe Original   *Med Versache*
                            Seite:
                            Heft: 1.2.1973

Document 5: Record from Nazi Archives at Bad Arolsen, Germany. Released by treaty to International Tracing Service and the U.S. Holocaust Memorial Museum, 2008.

Ariane Scriabin Knout (1910–1944): Russian daughter of composer Alexander Scriabim known as "Regine" in the Resistance *Armée Juive*.[1] Remained in Toulouse after France fell, converted to Judaism, and led one of the most active resistance groups in France until she was murdered by the *Milice*[2].

CR

A SUDDEN CONVERSION

I.

I had many names—Sarah-Ariane-Scriabin-
Fixman-Knout. Call me *simplement*
'*Régine*,' my resistance name. I knew
the aristocracy of Europe—musicians,
painters, government leaders. I danced
with them all. I am Scriabin's daughter,
schooled in music, art, languages.
But it had no meaning.

Until now.

War has come. I have studied, converted,
taken the name Sarah. I am a Jew. I say
to my husband who wants only safety
in Switzerland. "*Va-t-en. Je veux être
du côté des victimes.*" Here is my place.
Here are my children. Here I will bear
the first to be born a Jew. "*Va-t-en!*"

II.

Mother of four, leading hundreds,
passing information and money
over Garonne mountains, slipping
escapees through Toulouse
to the Pyrenees. Passionate, severe,
generous. "*Une véritable forteresse
juive.*"

---

1. *Armée Juive*: Jewish resistance group operating in France.
2. *Milice*: Paramilitary force of Vichy regime.

One small item in *La Dépêche Du Midi*,
21 July, 1944, four weeks before
the Toulouse liberation, 'assassinated
in Rue de la Pomme…enormous courage
and sang-froid'…by a young *milicien*,[2]
not yet shaving, showing his bravery,
doing his duty, who lived dutifully on.

---

2.   *milicien*: member of the *Milice*.

Zofia Kossak-Szczucka (1890–1968): Two Polish women—Zofia Kossak-Szczucka, a well-known Catholic writer and Wanda Filipowicz, a well-connected Socialist, formed Zegota (The Council for Aid to the Jews) in 1942. Zegota lasted until 1945 saving thousands of lives. Israel declared Zegota Righteous Among the Nations in 1963.

಄

ZEGOTA

Just the two of us in the chaos
of ghetto round-ups. Zofia and Wanda,
Wanda and Zofia, begging parents
for the children, catching them as they
were thrown. Every day, we came
here for the children. *Umschlagplatz.*
A quarter million deported, ripped out

of the heart of Warsaw. We had many
names, changed as often where we slept.
Veronika, they called me. Alicia, they called
Wanda. Also with us—Irena Sendlerowa—
the Gestapo broke her legs, her feet, every
bone. She never talked, never healed.

We found other tiny ones starving,
hiding in the ruins. Put them in carts,
covered them, pushed past guards,
our eyes straight ahead beyond ghetto
walls, out of starvation to the other side.
Christians, Socialists, Jews. Only a few

joined us to help. We called it Council
for Aid to Jews. Finally just *Zegota.*
Money by courier. Medicine, forged
papers parachuted like manna from heaven.
Feeding, saving anyone we could.
We, too, were betrayed, sent to Auschwitz;

the others shot. We tried to return.
Our country did not want us. Threats.
Interrogations. Forced into a life in exile.
Finally, a place for us. *Yad Vashem.* Trees—
carob, pine, olive—each leaf a memory.
Light glimmers along a scented path
with our names—Zofia, Wanda, *Zegota.*

Madeleine Dreyfus Levy (1920–January, 1944): French granddaughter of Alfred Dreyfus fled Paris with her family and joined the resistance helping Jews escape to Spain. She was betrayed and died in Auschwitz.

CR

IN A QUIET CORNER

of Montparnasse Cemetery, it is difficult
to find the headstone. Crowded among
lavish crypts, the simple Dreyfus grave,
pitted concrete worn flat, a few dead
flowers, almost hidden on *allée* 28.
There, just the carved names.

Of course his famous one first.
Just beneath his, hers: "*A la mémoire
de Madeleine Dreyfus Levy, deportée
par les Allemands, disparue à Auschwitz
à l'âge de 25 ans.*" She and her grandfather
often walked these streets—he, already

stooped by trials and prison; she,
the bright grandchild who clapped
at his songs, giving him joy the past years
had cheated him. Never late, wreathed in
silence, almost a perfect *résistante*.
Except for a deaf right ear.

Day job—*Secours National*;[1] night job—
Combat[2]—raising money, organizing food
and false papers, planning escapes through
passes in the Pyrenees. Working
through the night knowing she was hunted,
running back to pack a few warm things

to take into hiding. Never hearing
the concierge trying to warn her or the *Milice*
entering. The others were released. Only Mlle,
with the well-known Jewish name, shipped
to Drancy's flood-lit filth. Convoy 62,
Eichmann approved, arriving Auschwitz

---

1. *Secours National:* National social service agency of France.
2. *Combat:* Resistance newspaper and organization.

three days later, cold November, 1943.
One of the few to avoid immediate selection,
shaved, disinfected, everything stolen
but a number—#69036. It took only
a few months. January, 1944, typhus,
red-spotted. Seventy pounds, delirious.

Death. Years spent tracing what happened.
Longer for the medals to come—
Médaille Militaire, Croix de Guerre
avec Palme, Médaille de la Résistance.
Doing her duty. Like her grandfather.
Two names in a quiet corner of their country.

Bluma Lichtenstajn: poem and name are a composite from testimony and diaries of women locked in Poland's Lodz ghetto (1940–1945) who resisted by working as slowly as possible. Most of the women who did not starve or freeze to death died from epidemics or were murdered at death camps such as Chelmno.

CR

ARBEIT MACHT FREI [1]

Trapped in this filth without food,
water, sewers. Work, Rumkowski[2] says,
work! Never enough to eat. A few rotten
potatoes. Hours waiting to wash scraps.
It is only a matter of time.

Walls twelve feet high, more locked
in every day. Taking others away.
We hear a new word, Chelmno.
This winter worse than the last.
It is only a matter of time.

Yesterday, Spiegel died. After
eating his whole family's portion.
This morning, they took them all.
Already two families have moved in.
And then it will be their turn.
It is only a matter of time.

Rumkowski gives orders. 'Work,
Bluma,' he says, 'work day and night.'
I work, yes, I keep working,
as long as I can. In wet clogs,
always wet clogs. Even my feet
weep. Ice and mud everywhere.

Twelve hours shifts. Lice bite,
bleed us to death. I work
as slowly as I can—only one
mattress cover will they get from me.
I leave holes, make sure it will
come apart. Let them freeze,

---

1.   *Arbeit Macht Frei:* "Work will free you" sign at entrance to many German death camps.
2.   *Mordechai Chaim Rumkowski:* Controversial head of *Judenrat* (Jewish Council required by Nazis) of Lodz ghetto.

their beds rot. I do not let
them see my feet, my bleeding
fingers. Yesterday I fainted.
A woman picked me up. I do not
know her. I must try to find, thank
her. They would have taken me.

My husband is gone. He said
they would take the men first.
Women would be safer. Hah!
Struggling to stay alive by
working. Slowly, always slowly.
It is only a matter of time.

Zivia Lubetkin Zuckerman (1914–1978): One of the founders of the Polish resistance group ZOB (*Zydowska Organizacja Bojowa*/Jewish Fighting Organization), she fought in Warsaw ghetto uprising and escaped to Aryan side as Nazis burned the ghetto in May, 1943. After the war, she moved to Israel and was a witness at the trial of Eichmann.

CR

ZIVIA REMEMBERS *UMSCHLAGPLATZ*

Umschlagplatz—ugly word, ugly
place. Look. Almost nothing remains
of *Umschlagplatz*, in the middle
of Warsaw, the middle of Poland,
the middle of a ghetto, the middle
of the starving world of Jews in
the middle of the twentieth century.

Now only a wall, a plaque, a few dead
roses. So little to remember so many,
each soul herded here. Twelve thousand
a day in the blistering heat of summer,
1942. Doctors, lawyers, dancers,
children. Freight straight to Treblinka,
human cargo to be murdered.

We had no help, nothing, and yet,
how could we not resist? Remember
as you leave the square's dying roses,
how we fought—anything we could find
or make—sticks, knives, iron pipes,
light bulbs with sulfuric acid, a few guns.
Never enough, yet we fought and fought.

Nazis burned everything. To leave no
evidence. But there were sewers.
Lower and lower we went swimming
our way out with rats and garbage
to bear witness, to remember those
who chose to stand and fell, fighting
in the blistering heat at *Umschlagplatz*.

Schendel Margosis (1902–1986): Born in Ukraine, moved to Persia, then to Belgium before war began. After her husband fled to Portugal, Schendel Margosis fled with their children to France in 1940. She risked her life numerous times until she and her children crossed the Pyrenees to Spain in November, 1942, and eventually settled in the US.

☙

SCHENDEL MARGOSIS' *LUKSHEN*[1]

"*Lukshen,*" she called her poker winnings
and black market cigarettes, warning
the children, "*touche pas*" in broken French.
Gathering, hoarding, preparing for any chance
out of the charnel house with barbed-wire quotas.

Lucky children to have a well-traveled
mother. Russia, Persia, Palestine. Finally
Belgium before that May when the bombs fell.
Lucky to get on the train. Traveling south.
Always south. Seven days of strafing, stopping,

crawling. Until Cazères when the train died.
Sleeping in barns, a refugee camp in Toulouse.
Always the danger of being rounded up. Knowing
when to walk out again into the night. Always
moving, finding their way to Marseille slums.

Safer among rats, bugs, criminals. The "*lukshen*"
hidden—Pralines, Lucky Strikes, pure sugar—
waiting to be traded for black market dollars.
Finally papers allowing a trip to the Pyrenees
mountain air to cure her 'sickly' children.

A walk as evening fell, the lucky approach
by two "*passeurs.*" Their demands. Her terror
and risk. Forty thousand dollars to follow
strangers over boulders, into chasms. Her short
legs and stout body struggling over rocks,

---

1.   *Lukshen*: noodles in Yiddish.

dirt and snow, scrambling higher when they heard
dogs and German shouts. Schendel Margosis,
three children, two strangers, never looking
down, scraping their way over. Lucky children,
her *lukshen* buying them a soft pink Spanish dawn
        and an American life.

Rita Levi-Montalcini (1909–present): Italian neurophysiologist who, after graduating from the University of Turin Medical School in 1936, continued her research in hiding. She won the Nobel Prize in Medicine in 1986 for the discovery of the neuron growth factor.

CR

Dr. Levi-Montalcini's Passion

Science, questions and precision,
always her passion. A doctor,
just beginning her research
as Italy's doors slammed, labs
shut. Signs nailed on every
street, demanding neighbors shoot
anyone suspected of being a Jew.

And still the passion, setting
up a make-shift lab in the bedroom,
incubating chick embryos, silver
staining, sealing in paraffin.
By candlelight, slicing with
a microtome, comparing nerve
cells as bombs fell and shattered.

And still the passion. Lugging
the Zeiss microscope, ophthalmic
scissors, watchmaker's forceps
to the basement during nightly
deafening hours. Women praying;
children crying; she, a doctor
cradling slides, pondering neurons.

Moving the passion to the hills
to escape Turin rats and rubble,
setting up another lab on a tiny
table, begging farmers for fertilized
eggs, 'better for the babies,' she said,
but she had no babies, always working
alone, carried by questions, passion

and neurons just beginning
to differentiate, cell from cell,
spinal column from ganglia,
wondering what and how, studying
through the night, coming nearer
to seeing, closer to uncovering
what she would call "growth factor"

and maybe, out of the lugging
and begging, the confinement
and isolation, out of the will
to ignore hatred and terror,
out of the passion to find beauty
in silver-stained slides, maybe—
for Alzheimer's, spinal cord
injuries, multiple sclerosis—
just a bit sooner, a cure.

Dr. Roza Papo: (1913–uncertain): Born in Sarajevo, she joined Josip Broz Tito's National Liberation Army in 1941, heading partisan hospitals. After the war, she became an infectious disease professor at University of Belgrade. The first female Yugoslav general, she received six medals of valor.

CR

General Dr. Roza Papo Reports from the Front

November, '41

Doctors, nurses, the wounded,
blindfolded when brought here.
Our hospitals known only
by code names. Someone always
following to cover trails
with tree stumps, branches.
This we have learned. Hide
everything. This hospital lies
buried between rocks and snow.

February, '42

We sterilize only at night
to hide the smoke. Stakes
are high; the fighting, vicious;
our partisan rules, severe.
The *Ustaše*[1] hunt the wounded
in hospitals, butcher monks
in monasteries, kill anyone
anywhere. This we have learned.
Hide everything.

---

1.   *Ustaše*: Croatian fascist collaborators who killed thousands of Serbs, Gypsies, and Jews.

July, '42

Our peasant women, seventy years
old, firing guns, crossing mountains
with wheat and eggs. Captured
and tortured by the *Ustaše*, yet
they escape, return to battle.
This we have learned. One hundred
thousand Yugoslav women *partisankas*—
determined to fight, will not stop.

December, '42

Who is worse? The Nazis or the *Ustaše*
who burn women with cigarettes,
delight in torture and pain. This we
have learned from partisans who escape
with entire bodies blistered. Not a spot
untouched. Heads forced into bags
of crushed horseradish, fumes
burning skin, destroying lungs.
Bodies contorted until bones break.
Only tragedy can be learned from this.

March, '43

Typhus everywhere. We warn, "*Only
snow, rain, never water from streams.*"
But they drink and return delirious.
So sick we think they cannot live
through the night. They roll in snow
until the fever breaks, their blisters
crust. This we have learned: there are
miracles. They rise, return to their village.

November, '43

Our soldiers must be thieves, raiding
German hospitals, stealing serum,
ether, chloroform. They arrive stinking,
supplies buried in manure carts.
We never have enough. I reset legs,
remove shrapnel, cut out bullets.
Sometimes a sip of *rakija*,[2] mostly
nothing. I have learned to do without.

February, '44

No one was prepared. No soldiers
had marched thirty kilometers in snow.
Peasants had never heard a radio
before. Or me, a doctor, what did I
know, just beginning. The *Ustaše* murdered
sixty thousand. Somehow, three thousand
partisans found us. We have been strong,
tied up twenty German divisions.
We have learned to endure. If we can
just hold on, the end must come.

---

2.   *rakija*: strong Slavic brandy-like drink distilled usually from fruit.

The role of women such as M. Pappailiou in the Greek resistance is still being researched by scholars.

ଔ

Andartissa Meni Pappailiou

She fought in the mountains before
coming to us, to *ELAS*,[1] our small group
just outside Athens. Older—she might
have been twenty-five—and the nicest

of the women, she arrived in her blue
lafiro,[2] the German uniform she took
from a dead Nazi. She also toted
his gun, would not give it up.

Dark eyes, short brown curls, she took
the resistance name, Thiella—'storm.'
We had a code of silence, were trained
not to crack if tortured. We never used

her real name, Meni Pappailiou. Thiella
was educated, from the city, a leader.
Exercise, training, drilling, discipline,
every day until night. Many of our women

were illiterate. She taught them to read
and write, these women who rose up
from villages, walked out of the mountains,
dropped fear into family fishnets

and joined us, convincing fathers, uncles,
brothers to let them go, forget their *timi*—
'worth,' or they came anyway. Women free
for the first time. To speak, face danger,

---

1. *ELAS*: National Popular Liberation Army (*Ellinikos Laikos Apelefherotikon Stratos*).
2. *lafiro*: looted goods.

death. We carried machine guns, wore
uniforms, braids only , no hair down
until liberation. We wrote slogans
on walls, shouted hope into *honakia*,[3]

gathered greens in the country for soup
to feed those who had gone underground,
those who were starving. When Greeks
died in the street, we buried them.

When people had nothing, we fed them.
When people wept from fear, we comforted
them. *ELAS* took us, trained us. We took
ourselves seriously. Greece, occupied for

so long by so many. Thessaloniki
and the north, by Nazis; the East, Bulgaria;
South, Italy, until the Nazis raped it all,
rounding up whole villages, killing

even as they retreated. Their cruelty
fueled us; danger fed us while the Nazis
starved us. Finally, the liberation, then
again war. The *Dhekemvriana*—'December

events,' 1945. Rapes, killings, street battles
everywhere. Greek against Greek, right against
left; resisters, now hunted by police, the British.
Particularly women who had found voice.

The Nazis were gone, the war was over,
yet still they fought, Greek against Greek.
Near Omonia Square, the center of Athens,
they shot Thiella, killed the kindest of us.

---

3.   *honakia*: crude bullhorns made of scavenged materials.

Liselotte Pilku (uncertain–1981), a German woman, married to an Albanian, whose family gave refuge to a Jewish family that had fled to Albania.

CR

REFUGE IN ALBANIA

Hitler was good for Germany. That's how I felt. After all,
I was German. Even after I married Njazi Pilku, a Muslim
studying in Germany and moved with him to Albania,

I never forgot the secret meetings with Hitler in the basement
of our house in Braunschweig. I framed a photograph of Hitler,
hung it in our living room in Durres on the Adriatic coast.

We lived by Albanian and Muslim laws—*Besa*, from the ancient
Albanian *Kanun*, a code of hospitality and tolerance.
"The house belongs to God and the guests." I practiced Moslem

rituals, covered my head, went to the mosque, fasted
during Ramadan, circumcised our sons when they were thirteen.
King Zog opened our borders, invited Jews to Albania.

We were a backward country. We wanted Jews, needed
them. From Germany, Austria, Yugoslavia, we took in all
who came. They were our guests, our two thousand Jews.

When the Gerechters fled from Hamburg, we protected them.
We fed them, moved them from our beach house to Tirana,
to the country, to the mountains, wherever they would be safe.

The Italians left us alone. It all changed in 1943 when
the Nazis came. They ordered all Jews turned over.
We refused, said we knew no Jews. *Kanun, Besa*—

if there was a knock at the door, we knew—take responsibility.
We organized 'liberation councils' to help our Jews. I didn't think
about the risk to me, to my family. They would have killed us.

The SS liked me. They came to our house often, laughed, boasted,
drank. We passed off our Jews as relatives from Germany.
Maybe the photograph of Hitler helped. But always, the danger.

The Gestapo searching homes, yelling in the street, hunting Jews.
I yelled back, *"Verschwinden Sie! Ich bin auch eine Deutsche!"*
("Leave us alone. I, too, am German.") And they left.

We lived by Albania's code. We kept our word, our promise.
It was our honor to protect our guests. More Jews would have
found safety. If only more had known, if only more had come.

Roza Robata (1923–1945): Polish resister who, along with Alina Gertner, Regina Safirstajn, and Esther Wajsblum, was hanged in January, 1945, just days before the camps were liberated, for smuggling gunpowder to aid the Birkenau uprising.

CR

Roza's Power

At Auschwitz, dogs and death had all the power
Beatings, pain and hunger, always ours.
No matter, twenty women took the *abfall*—the overflow powder.

Despite freezing terror, dogs, and crushing power
the women dared in the shift's last hour
to twist into their scarves tiny buttons of powder

and turn it over to others whose only power
was to pass it on. Out of despair and stupor,
under the guns of guards we took the powder.

After the explosion, silence is our only power.
There is nothing more they can do to us—Esther,
Alina, Regina, me—injecting us, burning us with powder,

smashing our hands to break us. The gallows tower.
It is almost over. Perhaps some will remember
what we did and did not do when others had all the power.

```
                      Au.Häftl.Nr.    24 961

    Name:     R O B O T A,  Rosa
    geb.
    em:            —      inf  —          Nat.:  —

    abgesandt am:      —                 Laborunter-
    eingegangen am: 18.8.1944            suchungen de:
                                         SS-Hygiene-
    einsendende Dienststelle: Beklei-    Instituts
    dungskammer Auschwitz                Auschwitz
                                         OCG 2/102
    Material:                            Ordner 306
    Ergebnis:                            Seite: 88

    Weitere Angaben siehe Original
```

Document 6: Record from Nazi Archives at Bad Arolsen, Germany. Released by treaty to International Tracing Service and the U.S. Holocaust Memorial Museum, 2008.

Rita Rosani (1920–1944): Italian teacher of young children in Verona before the war. She is the only Jewish woman partisan known to have died in combat in Italy.

CR

UNDER VERONA'S TREES

They are turning now—the chestnuts.
The leaves descend; the earth is warm,
warmer yet with the blood of our group,
smaller now because of the betrayer

who broke and led the enemy here.
Five hundred Nazis raging in defeat,
mixed with my country's own fascists,
against our fifteen partisans.

They have disappeared into the woods,
leaving us, the wounded, in summer's remains.
It is so still after all the shooting.
Lying here, I learn to live with wounds.

Something disturbs. Twigs snap. A face
above me, a gun, fine leather boots
of my country. He is young, too young
for this and yet his aim blocks the trees

beneath Verona's sea-blue sky.
The leaves still descend at summer's end,
the woods of Verona turn gold as my country
crackles and explodes. Roots wrenched

from Italy's forests, the trees must bury
in their rings the pain of children
and teachers. Their leaves will share
the earth; the wind must carry our souls.

Baroness Germaine Halphen de Rothschild (1884–1975): Part of the French branch of the family, Baroness Rothschild rescued 130 children from Germany after Kristallnacht. She brought them to her home in France and then paid for their passage out of Europe to America and elsewhere.

CR

THE CALL OF SHATTERED GLASS

The whole world heard it—*Kristallnacht's*
shattered cities, stores, lives. For most,
deafness and paralysis. Yet one petite
woman with dark eyes, her own Lalique
and Baccarat still untouched, gazed beyond

her beveled windows, imagined each
orphaned face, heard each small voice
calling. Paying any price to bring them
out of Germany, Czechoslovakia, Austria—
each child a jewel added to the Rothschild

collections. Mme gathered them into her
own Chateau de la Guette until Paris fell,
buying a hotel in the south, moving them,
feeding and schooling them in La Bourboule.
Leaving money for them when she, herself,

had to flee for her life, enough to bring
them out over the Pyrenees to Spain,
to fishing boats that would take them
to America. Tiny charges implored to say
only *oui* or *non* and smile when questioned,

only smile. After the war, Madame
would return to ransacked homes, crushed
chandeliers, stolen paintings. She would
search freight cars filled with her
belongings marked "Goerring for Hitler."

Some canvases could never be restored,
some heirlooms were never found—
precious possessions smelted for
the Reich. Yet one hundred thirty children
settled in other countries, learned new

languages, began again. Sixty years later,
they would return to Chateau de la Guette
from Boston, Miami, Cincinnati, Canada,
Israel, Australia. Strangers linked
by dim, grim details, coming together

to place a plaque for the Baroness
Germaine Halphen de Rothschild
who heard the call of shattered glass
and added to the Rothschild collection
irreplaceable, terrified treasures.

Emilie Pelzl Schindler (1907–2001: Born on the German-speaking border of Czechoslovakia, Emilie saved hundreds of Jews in the factory she and Oskar ran during the war and was finally recognized by the Garden of the Righteous in a ceremony in 1994.

℘

EMILIE'S LIST

Schindler's list is also Emilie's, though she
never knew who created it—might have been
Goldman, she said—three hundred workers
from the factory Oskar 'bought' from Jews,
seven hundred fifty from Plaschow, a few others.
Emilie Schindler, the tiny woman who married

Oskar and stayed despite the betrayals, who saw
her childhood friend, Rita, a Jew, murdered
on the street by Nazis. Emilie, who never forgot
and fought to save all on their list. Keeping them
alive is also Emilie's story. Alone, going to
the Nazi general—her old swimming teacher—

pleading for a permit to move the factory from
Cracow to safer Brunnlitz, moving everyone,
searching for food, selling jewels to buy on the
black market, desperate to feed thirteen hundred
Jews and keep the factory looking busy,
but making nothing. Rescuing Jews again

and again, again Emilie's story—the female
workers sent to Auschwitz despite all the bribes,
finally getting them released, returned, fragile
and emaciated, hand-feeding them her semolina
porridge until they gained strength. And the last
rescue of 250 Jews is also her story, mid-winter,

twenty below, packed in railroad cars, coming
from slave labor in Goleschau. A soldier pounding
her door in the middle of the night, telling her, 'Take
the Jews or we shoot them.' Using a soldering iron
to force open the frozen bolts. Pulling out the dead,
their eyes glowing like coals, the rest barely alive.

Carrying them into the factory-turned-hospital,
spoon-feeding them until they remembered how to eat.
And finally, twenty years after Oskar, Emilie's name
added to the plaque in the Garden of the Righteous,
after those she saved besieged *Yad Vashem* on her behalf.
Who else would have saved them, they asked. Only Emilie.

Sophie Scholl (1920–1943): German Sophie Scholl and her brother Hans created the resistance group White Rose. The organization was betrayed by a janitor at the University of Munich in 1943. After being beheaded by the Nazis, a scrap of paper with one word on it was found in her cell.

CR

ONE WHITE ROSE

What we leave behind
is not the night terror,
carrying pamphlets
through dark streets,
dropping them in corridors
to drift like snow
fallen before dawn,
or the day terror
knowing betrayal
could come at any time.

What we leave behind is
not rage at betrayers,
torturers, those who did
nothing, or those who
sentenced, raised
the ax, watched it fall,
not the awareness
of blood about to flow,
bones about to be severed.

What we leave behind
is but one word
freedom
on a scrap in a cell
and one white rose
laid upon frozen soil.

Zuname: Scholl

Vorname: .   Sofie

Mädchen-/Tarnname:

geboren am: 09.05.21

Geburtsort: Forchtenberg

Nationalität: —

Häftlingsnummer: —

Fundort: PP Mü-Stadelh 2498/230

— — — —

II   DC

Name: S C H O LL Sofie .... No: AL/9/10

Nee: 1922 .... Nat: . unknown ....

B. D: .... X Ref: ....

B. P: ....

Address: ....

Occupation: ....

Last news: executed at Munich-Stadelheim ....

Date: .... 22.2.1943 ....

Enquirer's name: ....

Address: ....

Relation: ....

Document 7: Record from Nazi Archives at Bad Arolsen, Germany. Released by treaty to International Tracing Service and the U.S. Holocaust Memorial Museum, 2008.

Genowefa Czubak/Sister Dolorosa (1904–1982), **Dr. Olga Goldfain** (uncertain–1974):
Dr. Goldfain, disguised as a nun from 1942–1944, traveled with Sister Dolorosa in Po-
land until the end of the war. Sister Dolorosa was named Righteous among the Nations
by *Yad Vashem* in 1980 (File #1851).

℃

WANDERING SISTERS

Once upon a terrifying time in Poland's
bitterest winter, Genowefa Czubak,

known as Sister Dolorosa of the Order
of St. Ignatius of Loyola, fell ill in the town

of Pruzana where there were no longer
any doctors except for Olga Goldfain who

was locked in the ghetto. Two nuns gave Nazi
guards a litre of vodka, found Dr. Goldfain

among frostbitten prisoners, took her to
the convent where she cured Sister Dolorosa.

One freezing midnight months later, in the tumult
of bodies pushed like potato sacks into cattle cars

headed for the ash piles at Auschwitz, Dr. Goldfain,
her head buzzing, bleeding from being beaten

by Nazi guards, ran from the tracks, begged for help
at the convent gates. Sister Dolorosa, already punished

for talking to a Jew when Dr. Goldfain cured her,
hesitated, prayed, slowly rose and searched

for an extra habit. Two nuns, Sister Dolorosa and
Dr. Goldfain, taking the name Sister Helena, walked

out into the night, into the lives of wanderers sleeping
in barns, living off alms and Sister Helena's mysterious

ability to heal the sick until 1944 when Sister Helena
removed her habit and became again Dr. Goldfain,

emigrating to Israel and Sister Dolorosa, expelled
from her order, removed her habit, and became

again a brave lay Catholic, Polish citizen, and
righteous rescuer named Genowefa Czubak.

Hannah Senesh (1921–1944) first woman parachutist in Haganah, parachuted back into her native country of Hungary where she was betrayed and murdered by Nazis.

CR

BLESSED IS THE MEMORY

AFTER HANNAH SENESH'S "AFRE HAGAFRU" (BLESSED IS THE MATCH)

Blessed is the memory of a woman who chose to parachute
back into Hungary to save others over her own safety in Palestine.

Blessed is the courage of a woman whom days of torture
could not break, who 'gambled on what mattered most' and lost.

Blessed are the bright, blue eyes of a woman who refused
a blindfold, locking her Nazi executioners in her steady gaze.

Blessed is the heart of a woman who had the strength
to stop its beating for her people and honor's sake.

Blessed is the whisper of a woman whose fierce legacy
beckons to the living from high on Mt. Herzl.

Blessed is the fire of a woman who knew no temporary
failure, who still kindles light in a dark world.

Blessed are the words of a poet who prayed that these things
never end: the sand and the sea, prayers for woman and man.

Recha Sternbuch (1905–1971): Recha and Yitzchok Sternbuch headed the Swiss effort to save Jews (*Schweizerischer Hillsverein für Jüdische Flüchling im Ausland*—HIJEFS) which supported hundreds of refugees. They also led the effort to save the Jewish refugee community in Shanghai and rescued 1200 Jews from Thereseinstadt. Recha Sternbuch continued working after the war to return to relatives Jewish children adopted in Nazi Germany.

ॐ

Bar Mitzvah Gifts

He, Avrohom, son of Recha and Yitzchok,
on this, his Bar Mitzvah day, receives
his *tallit*.[1] The men at *Etz Chaim*
Yeshiva[2] wrap the soft fringed wool
around him, blessing him.

Shacharit[3] begins—*Tehillim*[4]—psalms
and songs opening the heart to prayer.
The first *Kaddish*[5] as Avrohom looks up,
notices three young men he has never
seen before, not much older than he,

slipping into seats in the back, dirty
from crossing the border from France
hidden in the back of a truck,
walking three days without rest,
finding their way to the Yeshiva

Standing now for the *Amidah*,[6]
sacrificial and priestly blessings,
so familiar, so awaited on this special
morning, the second *Kaddish*, and then
the rabbi calling his name, "Avrohom"

---

1. *tallit*: wrap for covering shoulders during prayer.
2. *yeshiva*: school or, in this case, also synagogue.
3. *shacharit*: morning service.
4. *tehillim*: psalms.
5. *kaddish*: a prayer.
6. *amidah*: standing prayer.

as the Yeshiva doors burst open, snow
and wind blow in. Swiss police charge
down the aisle, epaulets and billy clubs
shining, shattering Sabbath peace,
surrounding the young men, yanking

them toward the door as the congregation
tries to continue to welcome Avrohom
to this moment, a youth listening with
a new ear, each Hebrew word sparkling
on this Sabbath morning, the rabbi

next to him, the older men undressing
the Torah, opening it to the week's portion
which he will read, but there is his mother
suddenly in the men's section arguing
with the police, insisting the police leave.

Avrohom sees the commotion as the youths
are dragged out. Recha and Yitzchok,
his parents, look back with sorrow,
wave to Avrohom to continue, and are gone
into another gust of frigid mountain air

as the rabbi taps Avrohom again to begin
blessing the Torah. It is the moment
his parents have waited for since he was born,
the moment of "*Baruch ata adonai*"[7]
as the Torah is laid upon fine white silk,

the *ner tamid*[8] aglow above, the sterling *yad*[9]
sparkling, the rabbi bending over him
as he begins to chant on the *bima*[10]
with the memory of a kiss in the air,
a wave from his parents, their eyes sad

---

7. *Baruch ata adonai*: Blessed are You, God.
8. *ner tamid*: eternal light above the bimah.
9. *yad*: pointer used to read from Torah.
10. *bima*: raised podium in a synagogue.

and frightened and proud, torn from
their son, the Yeshiva, from the Sabbath,
torn from holiness into the horror
of a torn world while he keeps reading,
right to left, chanting the familiar trope,

the men in the congregation nodding,
standing beside him, listening to his
Haftorah, aleinu, kaddish, Adon Alom,[11]
his mother already on the phone
to anyone who will answer on Shabbat,

willing to do anything to locate
the terrified refugees, finding help from
the Polish Embassy and, just in case,
the Papal Nuncio, his parents rescuing
the doomed youths as they were about

to be sent back across the border, bringing
them to Avrohom's celebration, long after
the last prayer, the holiest Bar Mitzvah
gift Avrohom would ever receive,
Pikuach Nefesh,[12] saving three lives.

11. *Haftorah...Adon Alom*: sections of a full Sabbath morning service.
12. *Pikuach nefesh*: saving a life.

Corrie Ten Boom (1892–1983) Dutch woman who survived several prison camps and Ravensbruck to become a Christian missionary after World War II. Her home in Haarlem, Holland is now a museum describing her life, her family and their bravery during Nazi occupation.

~

THE SAVING WALL

One by one they came, finding the way
to the *Beje*, our old, crooked house
on *Barteljorristraat* in Haarlem. Beaten,
bedraggled, terrified, most we moved

to safe houses until none were left.
Then we hid our "guests" with us,
crowded them above our little shop
with the sign: Ten Boom, *Horloges*, 1837.

"How should a Christian act?" I asked
myself when the war began, and heard
my father's voice, "With your heart."
So our family began small efforts until

the Dutch underground found us, offered
fake identity papers, forged signatures,
a 'Mr Smit' to build the wall (everyone
was 'Smit' in the underground). Without

a secret room, he told us, we were
a danger to all. Smit chose the back wall
of my bedroom. Safest, he said;
brick, he insisted. Wood sounded hollow.

Nazis would find the Jews in a minute.
And high, on the top floor, with buzzer alarms
in the rooms below. Six days his workers came
with "clocks to be repaired," bringing a few bricks,

hammers, packages of plaster, paint. Smit copied
the ancient molding exactly, chipping here,
peeling there, streaking the new wall's paint
to match centuries' old grime. Bookshelves

on the false wall, sagging with blistered,
water-stained wood. A sliding panel beneath
the bottom shelf, two feet wide, opening
into the secret room—just enough for a cot.

One person could lie down at a time.
A concealed vent for fresh air. Water stored
in jugs, hardtack, and vitamins. First came
Cantor Mossel. We called him Eusie; then Jop,

our apprentice; Henk , a lawyer; Leendert, a teacher
who installed our warning system; Thea Dacosta,
Meta Monsanto, and Mary Itallie, older, noisily
asthmatic. We practiced until our "guests" could

dive into the hiding place in seventy seconds.
We rehearsed delaying tactics, preparing
for the worst which came, February, 1944.
I was shivering with flu when their axes chopped

through floors, walls. Shouting, "Where are the Jews?"
they hit and shoved us down the stairs, dragged
my father, sister, and me to the Gestapo, then
to freezing isolation at Scheveningen prison.

Sleeping on reeking straw, I wrapped my coat
around me. Hearings, interrogations, always
answering, 'We have no Jews.' Pleurisy, fever.
Trying to control my thoughts. My only friend,

an ant. I fed it crumbs, watched it every day.
It kept me sane. One day in March, a smuggled
message, 'The watches in the closet are safe.'
What joy, knowing the hidden Jews were safe.

They had stood for days in the dark, cramped
space, not daring to move until the underground
rescued them. The wall saved them, not us. May,
after ten days in prison, my father died. June, 1944,

my sister and I were transferred to Vught Camp.
Every day, shots of the firing squad, then the boxcars,
eighty of us unable to sit, breathe, three days
without food to the bleak barbed wire of Ravensbruck.

Barracks 28, among hunger-bloated stomachs
and stick limbs of others, I was prisoner 66730,
crammed in, forgotten. Slave labor at Siemens,
unloading heavy metal rods eleven hours a day.

My sister, exhausted, another among the ninety
thousand women murdered there. I began to minister
to the sick, taking pages of a smuggled Bible
under my dress, reading to them among rats and fleas.

Until *Entlassen*, my release by a clerical error,
Christmas Day. The long trip home on swollen legs,
staggering into a hospital in Holland. They bathed
my scab-crusted skin, put me to bed, taught me

how to eat, to live again. I began to preach,
to try to heal those, like us, who had suffered
so much. I traveled from church to church.
After a speech one day in Munich, a man

stuck out his hand to shake mine, asking
for forgiveness. I recognized him—
the mocking guard who laughed at our naked,
sick, stick figures in the showers

at Ravensbruck. I stared at him, unable
to move, praying. When I finally lifted
my arm and offered him my hand,
only then did the war finally end.

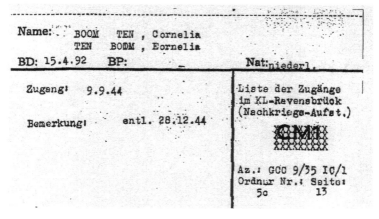

Document 8: Record from Nazi Archives at Bad Arolsen, Germany. Released by treaty to International Tracing Service and the U.S. Holocaust Memorial Museum, 2008.

Magda Trocmé (1901–1996): Along with her pastor husband and the townspeople of largely Protestant Le Chambon-sur-Lignon, France, M. Trocme gave refuge to thousands during WW II. The entire town was recognized for bravery by Yad Vashem in 1990.

☙

Whirlwind on a Windswept Plateau

Magda Trocmé, mother of many thousands,
social agency of one, spine of Le Chambon-
sur-Lignon. One terrified refugee whispering

to another, finding the way to the wind-swept villages,
a strong-willed woman, her pastor husband
with the gift of stirring speech, the two

and the towns that protected their hidden Jews.
Mayors, farmers, teachers watching from the granite
church towering above icy hairpin curves

that gave warning as the Vichy police approached.
They do not talk much about it, the townspeople,
descendants of Huguenots, with memories of their

own persecutions. Resisting occupiers, collaborators,
and their own terror to give others shelter.
Turning no one away, Magda Trocmé, daring to present false

identification cards to feed all at her table,
even after police arrested her husband—this tall,
straight-backed whirlwind of a woman, bare head

topped by braids, simple sweater, brown skirt,
fierce pacifist fighting for every life,
leading a tiny village to great heights.

Monica Massy-Beresford de Wichfeld (1894–1945): Born in England, she married a Danish aristocrat, moved to Lolland, Denmark and became a leader of the Danish Resistance until captured by the Nazis. She died of malnutrition and pneumonia in a German prison.

∽

Monica de Wichfeld: *Nej* (No) before *Ja* (Yes)

No, she said, to the lie that Denmark was neutral.
No, she said to her upper class life, the dances and parties that she loved.
No, she said to the occupation, joining the resistance, taking the lead
　　　in Lolland and Falster.
No, she said to safety, lending her rambling yellow mansion to the underground
　　　as a safe house for downed parachutists, her Maribo Lake for arms
　　　drops.
No, she said, to collaborators, burying guns in the woods, hiding explosives
　　　in her attic, sheltering Jews desperate to escape to Sweden.

No, she sensed, about 'Jacob,' the resistance worker sent to her, not trusting
　　　the man who would betray her and forty others.
No, she said, after betrayal, knowing she was hunted, refusing the underground's
　　　offer to transport her to Sweden.
No, she said to resistance members worried about her safety, stating she would not
　　　live a life 'at anything less than at a gallop.'

No, she said, to the storm troopers who kicked down her door before dawn
　　　in January, 1944.
No, she said to her Nazi captors, as she took her time to dress in cashmere
　　　and brown tweed, polished brogans.
No, she said to her guards, during ten-hour interrogations, wearing out
　　　her interrogators during months in solitary isolation.
No, she said, to her brutal environment, earning the whispered title of
　　　'queen of West Prison.'

No, she said to despair when the underground's plan to rescue her failed.
No, she said to continued isolation, tapping notes in Morse code
　　　through the prison wall.
No, she said, at her show trial, powdering her nose as the judge read
　　　her death sentence, the first for a woman in centuries.
No, she said, when told she alone could ask for clemency, not the men
　　　arrested with her.
No, she said, when she learned that general strikes would occur
　　　among Danes if she were shot.
No, she said when her captors demanded she write a formal request, penning
　　　a note for clemency on prison toilet paper.

No, she said to the German guard who bowed to her as she was transferred
   to prison in Germany four days before D Day.
No, she said to the soiled blankets, filthy mattresses, bedbugs, unbearable
   itching, forced labor, and vicious *Wachtmeisterin*[1] in prison.
No, she said to suffering, as she taught English, Italian, French history
   to younger women prisoners, making small gifts to comfort each.
No, she said to the final descent into hell on the cattle train three days, three nights
   freezing, without water, without food.
No, she said, to the death march in deep snow to Waldheim prison
   in bitter January, 1945.
No, she said, fighting the fever and pneumonia that ravaged her
   just after the Yalta Conference sealed the end of the war.

Yes, she finally whispered to the moon as she lay dying in prison
   in February, 1945.
Yes, oh yes, she would have said to Count Bernadotte of the Swedish Red Cross
   who brought all the Danish and Norwegian prisoners home six weeks later.
Yes, oh yes, she would have said to liberation dancing in the street in May, 1945.

Yes, oh yes, and what a dance she would have done.

---

1. *Wachtmeisterin*: low-level female prison guards

Mala Zimetbaum (1918–1944): Arrested in Antwerp, Belgium in 1942, she became a courier and translator at Auschwitz until she escaped on June 24, 1944, remaining free for two weeks. Recaptured, tortured, and brought for public execution, she cut her wrists and slapped her German captors with bleeding hands before being sent to the gas chambers.

CR

A Public Death, Still Chosen

My friends, I whisper, you must believe in
freedom coming closer. Two weeks we walked—
farms, villages, forests, almost to the border.
Rivers rush with it, leaves toss it in the air.

I have seen it, felt it everywhere.
So they brought us back. Soon all will know.
Chambers, death and dogs. The world will not
want to know; they will be forced to know.

So this is how it ends, a last unfinished hour
under a bit of sky. Lifted from bug-infested straw,
dragged from stifling Block 11. I cannot walk
after what they have done. Now gallows, a public death.

Torture was not enough. As if one more death
matters. Yet I will resist again. So little
remains mine—wrists, a blade hidden in my hair,
a last bit of energy. "My friends, come closer.

See the cuts quickly made, my blood spurting free,
splattering the executioner's face. Jewish blood,
red, warm, free. Look. Freedom comes. Watch
mine as I choose everything and need nothing.

CR

PART THREE
Picture Gallery

"For I have seen violence
and strife in the city"
(Psalm 55:10)

Photo 1: Friedl Dicker-Brandeis as a student at Weimar Bauhaus. Courtesy of the United States Holocaust Memorial Museum Photo Archives. (See p. 10.)

Photo 2: Marianne Cohn at mountain chalet retreat of *l'Armée Juive*. Courtesy of the United States Holocaust Memorial Museum Photo Archives. (See p. 14.)

Photo 3: Portrait of four Slovak women; Gisi Fleishman is second from left. Courtesy of the United States Holocaust Memorial Museum Photo Archives. (See p. 23.)

Photo 4: Zivia Lubetkin Zuckerman testifies during the trial of Adolf Eichmann. Courtesy of the United States Holocaust Memorial Museum Photo Archives. (See p. 34.)

Photo 5: Schendel Margosis (second from left) with children (Willy, Anna, Michel) in Brussels just before World War II. Courtesy of Michel Margosis. (See p. 35.)

Photo 6: Liselotte Pilku (second from right) with Jewish refugees at their home in Albania. Courtesy of the United States Holocaust Memorial Museum Photo Archives. (See p. 44.)

Photo 7: Hannah Senesh in the garden of her home in Budapest. Courtesy of the United States Holocaust Memorial Museum Photo Achives. (See p. 56.).

Photo 8: Portrait of Magda Trocmé. Courtesy of Nelly Trocmé Hewett. (See p. 63.)

Photo 9: View of Auschwitz-Birkenau in the winter. Courtesy of the United States Holocaust Memorial Photo Archives. (See p. 82.)

Photo 10: View of Auschwitz-Birkenau through barbed wire. Courtesy of the United States Holocaust Memorial Museum Photo Archives. (See p. 82.)

Photo 11: Mother and her children in Auschwitz-Birkenau. Courtesy of the United States Holocaust Memorial Museum Photo Archives.

PART FOUR
Epilogue

"Let them vanish like water
that flows away"
(Psalm 58:8)

HEADING EAST

These gentle hills I've so long loved
bear somber limbs I've never seen.
Is this because I've never been
when skies are wounded breast of dove,
when rivers flow like cooling lead,
fields lie cindered on ashen ground,
sunflowers without sun, bent, brown,
heads drooping over silent dead?
Or is this the way it looked that fall?
Trains racing east, smoking zinc, a
people shoved like beasts in a stall
never to see Paris again pink…a
slaughter…September rain…a pall…
Bear witness…Remember…Treblinka.

"Rough Justice"

The Rhone whispers cool and green,
flowing fast past Credit Suisse.
where high-hung tapestries welcome
clients, sculptures rise above customers.

Open an account, desire a loan, check
a deposit box? *Oui, si, da, yes,*
elegant employees whisper with a smile,
without accent. Multi-colored brochures

describe "*l'Art Integré*," the bank's
collection, exhibits, commitment
to cultural life—literature, painting,
photography. Just a bank doing its

civic duty, say the brochures, stacked
on Rue Monnaie. La Tempesse, a statue
of angled, silvered steel gleams
beneath a Renaissance canvas, shielding

elevators to 'Private Banking.' Calmos,
a torqued half-giant, towers above customers.
Exposed steel, head bowed, he keeps his
one eye on clients. A bank collecting art,

like the billions stamped in bars, stacked
in vaults. Objects smooth and quiet,
unlike the noisy ones who came again
and again without pre-war deposit slips,

without Auschwitz death certificates,
those whose only proof was a memorized
account number, whispered before another
disappearance. "Rough justice," they call

the settlement, after the long wait for
the slow return of soiled property, a pittance
for years of slave labor. Five decades
of waiting for the Rhone to whisper '*yes.*'

ONLY SEPTEMBER

In Krakow, a fellow traveler ran to a store
and bought us gloves—warm, soft, blue,
Polish wool gloves. *"It's only September,"*

I said. *"You might need them,"* she said.
The wind off the steppes crackled. Frost glazed
the tracks that one fed the daily frenzy, sparkled

on barbed-wire spikes taut around Birkenau
barracks. Ice webbed the green-yellow marsh pits
which still, occasionally, disgorge bones. It as only

September. The sky hung clear and cobalt above
Block 11's soot-black shooting wall; glass cases
spilled with *tallitot,*[1] their blue stripes and still-knotted

tzitzit[2] gathering dust on concrete floors. You know
about the mountain of twenty-five thousand pairs
of shoes, the mounds of glasses, the bite of wooden

clogs, frozen feet, and gas. You have heard of
crumbling crematoria, *Kanada*'s towers of blankets
and clothing stolen as starving people froze.

Now it is winter. At I pull on my soft blue gloves,
tug each finger into a perfect fit and look up
at naked trees and a bit of smoke curling far away,

I raise a fist covered with soft Polish wool
to shield against the sky's glare, blinking back
memory of the wind when it was only September.

---

1. *tallitot*: Hebrew. Fringed prayer shawls worn during religious services.
2. *tzitzit*: Braided fringe at corners of a tallit.

I NEED TO MAKE A PLACE FOR THEM, TOO

How important to read of heroes,
women and men who blow up tracks,
slip through the night with grenades
and supplies, survive in sewers and forests,
bear all burdens to bear witness.

How reassuring it is to think of these
stories when I stand between crumbling
crematoria and moss-covered ash pits
in damp dead air. How good it feels
until I see that I must also look

down at the stones, not only up
where a grey chimney still towers
or beyond where concrete still stands.
It is also necessary to look down
where plaques speak of a million

and a half who sang holding the hands
of children, who chanted softly
to the old, who prayed to a weeping
G-d as they were shoved and spit upon,
who faced the descent with dignity

and grace. Resistance of the spirit.
I need to make a place for them too.

TALLITOT[1] AT AUSCHWITZ

That cold September, the wind blew
off the steppes across Oswiecim,
but could not touch the thousands
of *tallitot* filling flass museum cases.

Black and blue stipes on white graying
like ash hung from crossbars; their *tzitzit*
lying in dust on the floor. Row after row
like guards, so many, unkissed, unworn,

just hanging in a silent room. The case reads
"Jewish fringed garments." I asked the guard
if they could be raised so the *tzitzit* wouldn't
drag in the dust. He shrugged. I asked the guide.

She shrugged. I wrote a letter to the director,
heard nothing. They are still there in those
musty cases, dangling above cell block 11.
Who can redeem them, those silent threads
hanging in the dust of what happened there?

---

1.   *tallitot*: Hebrew. Fringed prayer shawls worn during religious services.

STUTTHOF, LONG AFTER

You take the lonely road along the swampy coast
leaving behind Gdansk cafes, brightly painted amber
shops and Solidarity shipyards. You follow Route 7

through Kieszmark, pass circus tents in Stegna,
cross the Vistula before turning off toward barbed
wire and guard towers. Poland is flat, so flat, and this

brutal place so near the sea, you wonder why
it took the Russians so long to reach this death camp,
not liberated until May, 1945, after the murder of

thousands, mostly women, so many marched back
toward Germany in April of that year dying along the way
or shoved into the Baltic and shot. You have come to pay

your respects sixty years after. The crematorium
and gas chamber still stand at the end of a wide field
of barracks which in those days were crammed with

two hundred prisoners forced to sleep sitting up, never
allowed to lie down after slave labor, another form
of torture for the tortured, here where guards preferred

phenol injections to the heart rather than Zyclon B.
You walk through barracks filled with photos of
beautiful young prisoners murdered here, the dank smell

of mold and soot still rising from the little stove that couldn't
warm one human much less one hundred, wondering why,
so near the sea, so near the end of the war, the Russians came

so slowly while Nazi guards marched starving women
into swamps, threw them into the sea, still determined
to kill those who only wanted to live to see the killing end.

Pinkas Synagogue just before Sundown

The caretaker blinks the lights again,
but we cannot leave. Every Pinkas
Synagogue wall is covered with
delicately calligraphied names—Czech
towns in gold; last names of the murdered
in red; birth, and death dates in black;
each preceded by a gold *Magen David*.
Names of 77,297 Czech Jewish souls
meticulously gathered and inscribed here.

Outside in the early November dusk,
the ancient cemetery's jumble of tombstones
tumble and lean, layer after layer of Jews
who died centuries ago. But no tombstones
exist for these, murdered in our time, just
the names here, and above us, up narrow stairs,
thousands of drawings, collages, paintings
by children in Terezin who struggled to stay
alive and lost. Everywhere, shadows of the dead.

Soon we will head to the Spanish synagogue
for a Shabbat service. We will sit among tourists;
so few Czech Jews are left. How do you say *Kaddish*[1]
for a whole population? Impossible, but the walls
whisper names. Quickly, you copy as many as you
can—Berta Sagherova, Vera Schletterova, Marie Safir.
You tuck the sacred names into a pocket, keeping
them close, nod to the caretaker on the way out
to say *Kaddish* and a *shehechiyanu*[2] for American luck.

---

1. *Kaddish* is the prayer for the dead.
2. A *shehechiyanu* is a short prayer thanking God for "bringing us to this day."

WHEN HOPE WAS MINIMAL LIGHT[1]

(CINCINNATI SURVIVORS CLUB: THEIR POEM)

When hope was minimal light,
we survived. We survived
to know the happiness
of working free
into old age.

Do not expect lyric
lines or clarity. This is only
a translation, a stamp on stanzas
of dread. The inexpressible
we carry on our arms, in muscle
wrought from resistance.
This is all we can give
before we are gone.
Our history should be remembered
with the beauty and
thorns of red roses.

---

1.   Written as a group effort with their choice of words by 31 survivors on Feb. 21, 2001 in Cincinnati, OH, during a writing session with the Jewish Community Center's Friendship Club for Survivors.

Theta Museum, Bergen, Norway

For a moment you wonder whether it's worth twenty *krone*
to enter the dark alleyway between old red and yellow *Bryggen*
houses tilting toward each other and climb the rickety stairs

just to peak into the tiny cell where the Theta resistance group
worked. In the middle of Bergen under the noses of the Gestapo,
women like Wenche Stenersen Holm, men like Jan Dahm

and other students barely twenty years old tapped away day
and night on a small radio transmitter, tracking every activity
as German ships unloaded and refueled. From this hidden loft

in a wooden house on Bergen's wharf, they decoded and coded
messages to British intelligence and Norway's exiled government
in London. While friends wore paper clips in lapels to signal

resistance to Quisling and the German occupation, members
of Theta, knowing they were hunted, dressed simply, moved quietly
to avoid notice as they reported movements of the *Bismarck* and *Tirpitz*

until the ships were sunk, until a German soldier stamped his boot
in the office above the tiny room, collapsed the floor, and uncovered
the transmitter, ending Theta's efforts. Twenty *krone* to enter

Norway's smallest museum. Nothing compared to five bitter years
of German occupation with stomping parades, torture,
and executions, and the Norwegian bravery that helped end it.

A Woman Sifts at Chelmno

Dr. Lucia Pawlicka-Nowak's[1] long, pale fingers place in my hand the charred remains of a Mary Jane and a tiny cow, bits of its black and white spots still visible. "Touch," she commands in accented English, pointing to what has been unearthed here—the first mass gas killing center.

Her face is lined, chalky beneath jet black hair. She works mostly alone here at the small white museum almost hidden behind a church. Occasionally, a few schoolchildren come to help with the sifting. She is an archeologist who had a hunch, searched aerial photographs, hounded authorities for permission, and began to dig. As severe as her findings, she sifts earth, sorts and catalogues findings, pulls Jewish gravestones from Polish driveways, returns them to decimated cemeteries. Odd work for an archeologist. She is not Jewish.

A thousand a day, at least a quarter million murdered here. First everything stolen in round-ups, then starving in the Lodz ghetto, then transported here with any belongings still left. Some people they drowned in wells, some were boiled in quicklime. Not efficient enough. Then special vans built by Renault which could be hermetically sealed. Seventy could now be gassed at a time. Ten minutes with the engine running. Again too slow. The Nazis closed Chelmno after 350 days.

Case after case filled with their belongings. Bottles, buttons, lockets, charred spoons, pots, dentures with 1941 in Hebrew, pocket collections of tiny animals—a sheep, a goat, the cow I hand back to Dr. Pawlicka-Nowak. Sometimes, human remains are still found in in the digging. Then, rabbis are called to re-bury the bits of bone with care and a Jewish burial.

The sifter is quiet now, the run-off has returned to the land. We have passed lush farms, beet fields, trucks piled high with potatoes. Sycamores line the roads, children play in schoolyards. There are no Jews left in these towns. But still we have passed graffiti slashed across walls, swastikas dripping over Jewish stars.

The air smells of pine and hyacinth as we head to our car. The sun sets in a pink slant on a Polish archaeologist turning back to her work.

---

1.   Dr. Lucia Pawlicka-Nowak: A Polish archeologist who heads the research and museum at the Chelmno death camp. She is the Director of *Muzeum Bylogo Obozu Zaglady*.

FENCES AT BIRKENAU

It is only September, I keep telling myself, as I walk across the fenced, packed earth of Auschwitz-Birkenau from barracks to barracks. Wind and a cold rain slash at the dark wood hovels. Even before fall has begun, I cannot imagine surviving here. The average life span was fourteen days...if you passed *selection*.

Most women did not survive *selection* at Birkenau. As soon as Auschwitz II, as it is also called, was finished, a new rail spur fed directly into the camp. There would be no more delay marching those who had not died in the cattle cars directly to the gas chambers. Now they could be brought directly to Birkenau, unloaded to Mengele's music, and murdered. His viewing platform and the bandstand where prisoners were forced to play are still there. It is said Mengele particularly liked Wagner.

Everything went quickly here. In just a few seconds, belongings were stolen, sorted, disinfected, and made ready for redistribution to the Reich even before prisoners took a last breath. Three or four days in a stinking cattle car, then twenty minutes.

You cannot miss the ash pits, even in the rain. No longer white or grey, their green scum is the shade of moldy army uniforms. A few sharp reeds jut from the morass. One yellow weed struggles in one of the pits. Bone chips are mostly covered, but you know they are there.

It is an enormous undertaking to keep up this Museum, our guide tells us—the guard towers, the barbed wire, the barracks, the train tracks, crematoria. Finally the Germans have agreed to chip in for upkeep. Ten million dollars have finally been donated, but with strings. The money is earmarked for certain things. And reports must be filed quarterly. Attention to detail. A full accounting for every dollar.

The Germans cover the upkeep of the fences and guard towers. Barbed-wire fences. An enormous expense—twelve feet high, curved, zigzagged in wild patterns. Fifteen square miles bound by a jagged fence. At least a million and a half Jews were murdered here. Less than ten dollars a murdered soul. It is September. Birkenau will soon have to file its quarterly fence report.

The Silence at Treblinka

Treblinka was open barely a year. Enough time, though, to murder two hundred fifty thousand human beings. July, 1942 to November, 1943. Almost the entire population of the Warsaw Ghetto was shipped here. Forced into trains of terror and filth, rolling day and night. Sixty cars, one hundred human beings per car. Here, twenty cars-full could be murdered at a time—two thousand every two hours.

Just a day's work to the guards. Every single workday a guard could murder his quota of human beings and be home to play with his own children before dinner. First the Warsaw ghetto, then Jews from anywhere. Each a unique, terrified death. Just the beginning of Operation Reinhard—the final solution.

Now Treblinka is nothing but woods and stones. In September, it is already cold and windy, but the trees make no noise. The only sound is our own footsteps.

We walk quickly as they did—half a mile through the pines on a stone walk, then a slight turn to the left as they turned. There is no undressing house now, no dogs barking, guards yelling. Just more stones that suddenly turn jagged, jutting up. We have entered a stone forest—thousands of stones—each chiseled with the name of a village where every human soul was murdered.

These seventeen thousand jagged stones throw silent shadows all day long for 870,000 women, men, children murdered here in little over a year. Jews from the Warsaw ghetto, from Radom, from Lublin, from Bialystock, Slovakia, Greece, Yugoslavia. So many people in so little time.

August, 1943. The aborted uprising. Killing every one of the resisters. Then the hurried work to destroy all the evidence—burning bodies in huge pyres, crushing bones, burying ashes, plowing the ground under, planting trees and lupine. Three months later, a Ukranian peasant family was resettled here to farm the land.

Now, only stones, woods, a few elderly peasants gathering mushrooms. And questions. Who will atone for this? How many people would it take to atone? How long would it take to atone?

We stand a long time after saying *Kaddish*. No one moves. We listen to silence in a forest of stones.

Danube Shoes[1]

There are only shoes now, there
along the river beneath Budapest's
scarlet-roofed Parliament. A memorial
of shoes—women's, men's, work toes,
pointed toes, laces tied, untied, boot-tops
drooping like frozen leaves, blackened
by weather and time, hundreds along
the quay. And stones of mourners
paying respects in the spaces between.

Such a tiny monument to remind
of that long ago winter when suffering
under the Nazis wasn't enough.
The darkest days of 1944 and 1945, after
Eichmann's frenzied round-ups—hurry,
hurry, fill the cars, until 381,66l—half
of Hungary's Jews had, in one month,
been choked in Auschwitz chambers.

Eichmann's helpers, Hungary's own
Arrow Cross, continuing the terror,
pulling innocents from the frozen
ghetto, marching them to the Danube,
ordering them to remove their shoes
before the bullet and push into the ice-
clogged river, hundreds a day murdered
that way as the Russians marched closer.

This country that had courted the Jews,
claimed them as their own, until the Arrow
Cross turned on them even as Wallenberg
and Lutz were frantically trying to save them—
Hungary's own Fascists still up for beatings
and knuckleduster torture before the final
trip to the Danube, even as Hitler planned
his suicide; Eichmann, his disappearance.

---

1.   Shoe memorial on Pest side of Danube in Budapest, created by Gyuala Pauer and Can Togay
and dedicated in 2005.

It is important to come here, look up
at the castle, the steeples, the blushing
towers piercing the sky, and look down
as you walk beside the Danube on a quiet,
cold November morning before you bow
and leave a stone beside the shoes.

Two Glimpses of History

As we tramped the soft grass from marker to marker, the young mayor of Lidice answered our continuous stream of questions. We could not stop asking: Why did the Nazis burn the town to the ground? How many were killed? Did anyone survive? What happened after the Nazis left? It was the first site on the trip sponsored by the U.S. Memorial Holocaust Museum to death camps and World War II monuments and we wanted to know everything. Towards the end of the tour of the new Lidice, the mayor asked if we would like to talk with a survivor of the Nazi destruction of the village. We immediately said yes. So our small group trekked into the sparkling new town hall reception room and waited.

We were a group of fifteen—Museum supporters; religious leaders, Christian and Jewish; and a writer (me); with scholars accompanying us. I was writing about women who resisted throughout Europe during World War II when I heard about the trip to the Czech Republic and Poland. Ten death camps in ten days, seeing first-hand where so many had struggled to survive or perished, lectures at each site. I dreaded it, but signed up. I knew I had to see these horrific places. I tried to get my husband to accompany me. "You must be nuts!" was all he said. He had absolutely no interest. I, however, had to go, no matter how grueling, and was relieved, actually, to have a hotel room to myself where I could deal with my terror, horror, and, I hoped, have much needed quiet to cope with each overwhelming day.

We traveled first to Prague. Two trips to sites just outside Prague taught me more than thousands of hours of research could ever impart. Our first trip was to the small, now-rebuilt village of Lidice. The bus ride took no more than half an hour through the green, rolling hills of the Czech Republic. The Museum designed our trip to explore the full devastation of the Nazi years, including sites such as Lidice, only minimally connected to the near-destruction of European Jewry. So we began at this tiny village, wandering its sparkling white buildings, looking at markers, listening to the young mayor, taking notes. But it was the end of the afternoon that I will always remember.

Under a puff of silver hair, Mrs. Anna Nesporova walked slowly down the aisle of the large, sunny town reception hall and took a seat in front facing us. The mayor said he would be happy to translate for her. He told us Mrs. Nesporova wanted us to ask her questions. It would be easier that way, she had explained. She was short, plump, white-haired—a sweet looking woman. She wore a pink dress, a pin, a brown sweater. She smiled a bit and seemed relieved that several of us raised our hands.

How she survived the annihilation of this town and all its inhabitants near Prague is a long story, she began in Czech. A young bride, she was away giving birth in Prague hospital in June, 1942, when the Nazis randomly selected this idyllic Catholic mining village in the countryside of Bohemia for retaliation after Hitler's Reichsprotector, Reinhard Heydrich, was assassinated by the Czech underground. No one in the village was in any way connected to the assassination. It was just the Nazi way of retribution, of maintaining control through random terror.

But she was not there when they chose Lidice—nor when they rounded up everyone in the village. The men were shot in batches of ten behind the town's largest barn. First 192 men were shot; then, 71 women. The women in Lidice were made to watch the men die before being shot themselves or shipped to slave labor in Ravensbruck. The Nazis filmed each step of the destruction of this village as a training film—the shootings, the burning of bodies and homes, all evidence of a town burned into oblivion, plowed under. A training film. To help others learn to leave no traces behind.

Did any of the village children survive? Someone asked. A few, she said, those that looked Aryan enough were sent to Germany and adopted. Two of these children were found after the war and, after long negotiations, brought back to the village. Those that were a bit darker, a bit suspect, were sent to Chelmno or Auschwitz. They did not come back.

And her? What of her and her baby girl? The Nazis came to the hospital. They took her baby. She begged to keep the child. For that, they sent Mrs. Nesparova to Ravensbruck. For four years she endured slave labor, near starvation, beatings. Then the war ended and she slowly made her way back to the village that no longer existed. She returned to silence and absence. There was no record of her child or the town. Lidice had been completely razed and expunged from Nazi records. During her long months of slave labor, she knew nothing of her town, her husband, her child. She was driven to survive by the dream of someday reuniting with her family.

Slowly, the town was rebuilt and she resettled here. It was her home and always would be, she said. Did she find her child? No, she said. She still knew nothing about the baby who was taken from her breast. And her husband? Her then-husband had been murdered with the rest of the men of Lidice.

Yes, she like other survivors, somehow managed to resume life when the war and cruelty were over. Yes, she married again and had other children. But that one child, her first, she said with quiet dignity, she still carried in her heart. She looked out the window at the rolling fields and blue sky above Lidice, then turned back to us to say she had been searching for her for sixty years.

Anna Nesporova walked with us through the green memorial grounds, pointing to a large marble statue with many names, so many of them children, one of them, hers. On the way back to the bus, she held my hand, patted my arm. She said she was glad we came. She had one more thing to tell us, her translator says. "You must always try to be happy," she said, smiling.

As we climbed back on the bus, we could not take our eyes off petite Mrs. Nesporova who kept waving. And the new Lidice as the bus backed down the hill and turned toward Prague.

After tossing and turning throughout the night, I finally got out of bed before dawn to write everything I could remember about Lidice and Mrs. Nesparova. I climbed back aboard the bus at 9 a.m. I was already tired and we had been traveling only two days. We were still at the beginning of the trip. How was I going to keep going, I wondered. Then I thought of Mrs. Nesparova's sweet smile after all she had endured and told myself to get a grip.

We were again moving through the green Czech countryside, headed for another small village—Terezin. Not to see the village as it is once again, actually, but to get an idea of the prison, squalor, and courage of those who were imprisoned there. The bus pulled through high walls and dropped us on cobblestones in front of the fortress.

In a town that held 7,000 people before the Nazis took control, 50,000 Jews were crammed in together throughout the war years. Conditions were so bad and food so scarce that 16,000 Jews died from starvation and illness in 1942 alone.

And yet, Theresienstadt (as the town is known in German) was called the "model village" by the Nazis. It was used to dupe the Red Cross and the rest of the world not yet ready to know the true plight of European Jewry.

When information about the murder of millions of Jews began to leak out, the Nazis invited the Red Cross here to prove the stories of mass murder were untrue. Here they would show how well the Jews were being treated. It was the Red Cross visit that I wanted to replicate—the day that could have saved thousands of human lives on the edge of starvation and death, but didn't.

A big map showed the trail of the Red Cross delegation. I left my group and went on my own private journey. So much was built here for just for that one day when the Red Cross visited, here where the Jews of Czechoslovakia were rounded up and held, dying of illness or starvation, or until the Nazis deported them to Auschwitz. So much built for one false day in the midst of crowding, disease, torture, death. One day—July 23, 1944—when the Red Cross came.

I followed the trail taking notes, trying to imagine the thousands imprisoned here, particularly the children. It was the washroom with its dazzling brightness that stopped me short. I stood transfixed. Unlike the small, filthy fortress we had just seen where prisoners had to stand body to body until they grew rigid and died standing up—100 Jews per tiny cell without air or light. No, this bathroom had high, bright windows and space.

This bathroom's walls were tiled, still sparkling with shiny white squares. It had mock showers and sinks—clean, porcelain sinks—sixteen on each side of the long bathroom. I kept turning, watching my reflection above each sink's large, shining rectangular mirror. My reflection bounced back and forth in total stillness in this huge white room that looked like a camp bathroom built to keep campers healthy, but there were no campers here. Of the 15,000 children who passed through Theresienstadt, all but 100 were murdered or starved to death.

The Red Cross was led to this shining bathroom where they could admire its cleanliness. Then they were taken to the mock café where prisoners were forced to sit and smile as though enjoying a meal before being deported the next day. Then the delegation was taken to the bank that held no money, then to the school that taught no one. All false fronts built for the Red Cross visitors. Never, ever used.

You, too, can follow the path of the Red Cross delegation—the gardens through which they passed where "happy workers" watered roses and lilies (again, prisoners who would be deported to the death chambers of Auschwitz the next day); the false-front school building with "school holidays" nailed to the door (education was forbidden here although Jews risked their lives to keep teaching children in barracks); the soccer field where no game was ever played; the unused bandstand. You can follow each footstep of the delegation before they were fed a big lunch in the staff dining room, loaded on buses, and bid good afternoon.

I sat beside the Eger river for a while, trying to grasp the enormity of this tragic place. The Red Cross delegation's path carefully avoided the riverbank where I rested. Then the ash of 22,000 bodies blocked the flow. The delegation never saw the slow crematoria, nor the cells of the tortured.

You can look at the big map of Theresienstadt where the Red Cross path is marked in white and wonder why no one asked a question, why no one veered off in another direction, why no one got up from lunch early and suggested a walk. Why they bothered to come at all. You can stand in disbelief for hours in the huge white washroom staring at mirrors that saw Red Cross faces that never looked back.

I spent a long time in the Theresienstadt Museum. So many of Czechoslovakia's musicians and artists perished here or were shipped from here to gas chambers at Auschwitz. I stared at the score of *Brundibar*, the opera written by Hans Krasa that gave hungry children roles, taught them music, and raised their spirits. I stopped in front of the work of artist Friedl Dicker-Brandeis, Walter Gropius's favorite student, who found scraps of paper, bits of charcoal, anything to keep her students drawing, learning, hoping. The Jewish Museum of Prague holds 4,000 paintings of children that she hid in suitcases at Terezin just before she and her students were sent to Auschwitz where they were murdered in 1944. Theirs was a formidable type of resistance—resistance of the spirit, of the heart, of determination to create despite devastating conditions.

Prague is beautiful and vibrant; a city not to be missed. But these nearby villages also hold chapters of this country's history and tell the sad fate of so many of its citizens during the Nazi occupation. I will never forget Anna Nesparova's story of her lost daughter; Friedl Dicker-Brandeis' helping little Hanus finish the blue scraps of his collage, *The Sea*; or the children who sang their hearts out in *Brundibar*.

This is why I went on that journey and why I write about this era. Others have said, "Enough, already. Enough of the Holocaust." Well, for me, it wasn't enough until I stood in villages reading markers and names, listened to those who survived, saw the artwork of those who didn't, and had the opportunity to be touched by the reality of what Mrs. Nesparova, Friedl Dicker-Brandeis, and millions of others had to endure. And to learn from them—keep working, keep hoping.

STELLA'S STORY

I sit on the marble bench in the courtyard of Kahal Shalom synagogue in Rhodes. After rushing through crowded streets of this largest island of the Dodecanese searching for the synagogue, I want to rest in the shade a moment before entering. I let my eyes adjust from the dazzling sunlight.

Officially the sunniest place in Europe, Rhodes has already won my heart with its roses, the crenellated towers of the palace and city walls, and the clear azure water of the Aegean. I have only a few days in Greece which is not much time with so much history, so much beauty. I am most interested in the story of Greek Jewry, an important chapter of which is set here on Rhodes, the island of roses.

The first Jews came from the Holy Land, possibly as slaves, possibly as traders. As early as the first century BCE, the Apostle Paul found active Jewish communities throughout the Greek Islands, including Rhodes. The earliest Jews, who called themselves Romaniots, were influenced by Greek culture and language. Another influx of Jews, invited by the sultan Bayazid II to settle in Turkey, came east from Spain and Portugal after the expulsions and Inquisition of the fifteenth century. The newcomers brought with them Sephardic culture including the Ladino language. At its peak, the Jewish community of Rhodes exceeded 4,000, dropping during pre-war shortages to about 2,000. Until the Nazis came.

The synagogue is located in a shady courtyard in the old part of Rhodes town, just beyond a city square where a fountain splashes. The square has been renamed the Square of the Jewish Martyrs and contains a monument to the tragic story of the island's deported Jews.

I can see the carved wood *bima* (*tevah* in Ladino or raised platform in English) in the center of the synagogue and the ornate crystal chandeliers hanging from the ceiling, but I prefer to sit and watch the light coming through vine leaves trellised above the courtyard. There is a lot to take in. After all, this is the oldest, still-standing synagogue in Greece. Built in 1577, its high arches tower over black and white pebbles set in intricate *cohlocki* (mosaics) below my feet.

A carved marble plaque with many names hangs to the right of the door like a huge *mezuzah*.[1] I read the names: Amato, Ascher, Capelouto, Rahamim, Soulam, and so many others. The plaque is in French, "*En mémoire des deux mille martyrs de la communauté juive* (In memory of two thousand martyrs from the Jewish community). It was placed there by a survivor, honoring his parents, sister, and all those of the Rhodes community who did not survive the Nazi round-ups and deportations that decimated the Jewish Greek population. In 1940, 77,000 Jews lived in Greece. Only ten to fifteen thousand survived the Holocaust. Of the more than 1600 Rhodians deported, only 151 survived.

A young man wearing a *kippah* (small head covering) darts in and out of the synagogue. Sent by the Athens Jewish community, he acts as caretaker and answers visitors' questions during the busy summer months. I watch him check information with a woman sitting on the marble bench. She is thin, elegantly dressed, and has short brown hair and a quick smile. She sees me writing and asks quietly where I am from. "Maryland," I tell her, "near Washington, D.C."

---

1.   *mezuzah*: small parchment scroll of passages from Deuteronomy affixed to the doorpost of some Jewish homes.

"I'm Stella," she says. "I was born here." She points down the small street beside us. She betrays only a hint of accent in her soft-spoken voice. "I come back from the States every summer to help out at the synagogue." I'm afraid to hear her answer, but I say, "I hope you left before the Nazis came."

"No," she says. "I was here. Right over there is where they herded everyone." She points toward the square behind us where the fountain splashes. I ask whether she wants to talk, letting her know I don't want to intrude. She nods and begins telling her story, the story of Rhodian Jews, Rhodeslis as they call themselves.

Before the war, this was a well-known Jewish community. There were four synagogues and the Juderia was an immaculate, white-washed, bustling neighborhood. Women baked sweet pastries and marzipan for the holidays. Before the holidays, the whole Jewish community washed the streets together and made sure that the synagogues sparkled. One of the oldest and proudest communities of the Diaspora, Rhodes was called Little Jerusalem.

By spring 1944, the Nazis occupied the island, and on July 20, they rounded up the entire Jewish community, telling them to bring their jewels and money because they were to be transported to another island. After being herded without food or water onto small boats that took more than a week to reach mainland Greece, Stella and other Jews from Rhodes and the island of Kos were crowded into the SS prison camp at Haidari. Stella says quietly, "Men and women begged for water, but were thrown gasoline by sadistic SS guards. Many of our neighbors died on the boats and were thrown overboard or died in Haidari."

Then the thirteen days as the cattle cars rattled toward Auschwitz in heat and darkness, crowded without space to breathe, food, water. Stella and her sister struggled to stay together at Auschwitz, where, she says, "I might not have survived except for the blessing of Madame Katz." Stella explains that if you couldn't understand what the Nazis demanded in German, you would be beaten to death or sent to the gas chambers. Madame Katz and her daughter were from Belgium. They spoke French and Yiddish. With Yiddish, they could understand the German commands and translate them into French which Stella spoke.

Madame Katz mothered her own young daughter in this place of death and the twenty Rhodeslie girls as well. She stood guard over them throughout the tortured months in Auschwitz and the terrifying death march to Dachau. They survived the shootings, sleet and snow, exhaustion and starvation, reaching Dachau in April, 1945, the day before the camp was liberated by the Allies. Then came the months of regaining enough strength to reenter a world of loss.

"How could you come back here?" I ask.

"It was horrible the first years, "she says, "but I had no choice. It was my home. It gets a bit easier each year."

I ask my husband to take a picture of us. More than two hours have passed and I still haven't gone into the synagogue. "I have to go in," I say, although I want to stay beside Stella.

"Go," she says, "you must see it."

Another woman, who has apparently overheard our conversation, bends over toward us and says to Stella, "Thank you."

"For what?" Stella turns to her and asks.

"For surviving! I just hope you've had a good life—after all you went through," says the stranger before entering the synagogue. Stella smiles a bit, does not respond. I, too, keep silent, although I resent the interruption.

"I've got to go in. Will you still be here?" I ask.

"I don't know," she says.

I walk through the synagogue, stand before the intricate carvings, gaze up at the chandeliers glistening in afternoon light. Soft maroon curtains protect the Torahs. I stop a moment and say Kaddish, the prayer for the dead. It is the least I can do after Stella's story.

I wander into a side room that has been converted into a small museum. Photographs of pre-war life in Rhodes show laughing young men and women, groups singing on the beach, wedding pictures of handsome couples. I climb the stairs to glimpse at the women's section, but I am anxious to get back to Stella.

When I return to the courtyard, she is gone. No one seems to know where. But I have the photograph. My husband hands me the digital camera. She is smiling with her arm around me. I can still feel her presence.

I sit a moment longer, not yet ready to leave. No Colossus of Rhodes saved the Jews; no towers of the city walls protected them; no Knights of Rhodes came to their rescue. Here at the very end of the war, the Nazis, already losing, would not stop killing Jews. Most Greek Jews were murdered. The 151 Rhodes survivors were barely a remnant of the former Rhodes community of almost 2,000.

Now only 30 Jews live on the island. The twenty girls that Madame Katz mothered are scattered and Madame Katz recently died. That vibrant community is memory. But Kahal Shalom, Holy Congregation of Peace, still stands, restored and cared for with the support of American Express and the World Monuments Fund…and Stella and other survivors.

And Rhodeslis and visitors from all over the world come back. I was fortunate to come at just the right moment to sit beside a brave survivor and hear fragments of a tragic history. Stella's story is one of loss and life-long commitment to step through the pain onto the worn stones of the *cohlocki* and testify. Stella's story is what the Jews of Rhodes call a *cantica*—a Ladino song, filled with love and longing. Stella's story is a love story about a sun-splashed island and the shadow of its lost community.

Bar Mitzvah in Bordeaux

My husband and I walk along the banks of the Garonne River, passing restaurants and brasseries, checking out the menus for lunch. It is barely mid-morning in Bordeaux, but the chalkboards are already out, the streets cleaned, the old city's eighteenth century townhouses gleaming in the sun, the huge trees providing shade. Although the euro is falling daily, everything gleams in Bordeaux.

We make our way along the River and turn up toward the old city in search of the Grande Synagogue de Bordeaux. We walk along Rue St. Catherine through the city's pedestrian areas as French people stop at bakeries for a croissant on their way to work.

It is a Thursday morning; we doubt we will be able to enter the synagogue, but we have come to pay respects at this important place. Bordeaux was a hoped-for refuge for Jews during WWII who were fleeing other countries and Paris, hoping to board ships sailing out of the inferno. Some did escape that way. But most did not.

Bordeaux became one of the most important centers of Nazi police and military activities in occupied France. Not only were the Nazis interested in using the port, but vineyards and particularly the Rothschild holdings offered opportunities to feed Goering's appetite for expensive Lafite-Rothschild Bordeaux wines. And then there were the Jews—always the Jews to be rid of.

Jews had been in Bordeaux for centuries, many of whom settled in Bordeaux after fleeing Spain and Portugal during the Inquisition. During the Nazi occupation of Bordeaux, two-thirds of the city's Jewish population, refugees and locals alike, including residents of the Jewish old-age home, were rounded up; imprisoned at the Great Synagogue for days until the trains were ready to deport them to Auschwitz. Then, in January, 1944, French Fascists ransacked the Great Synagogue, looting and further desecrating the space. After the war, the remaining Bordeaux Jews spent years rebuilding this most beautiful and largest Sephardic synagogue in France.

We do find *Rue de Grand Rabbin Cohen* just off the main thoroughfare. There the synagogue stands—its huge stone edifice behind the gravel parking and outside entry area. The entire area is surrounded by a high wrought iron fence. On the fence are warnings—report anyone or anything suspicious people to the SPCJ (*Service de Protection de la Communauté Juive*).

A boy, his white collar open under a dark suit passes us and buzzes into the property. The gates open. "May we enter also?" I ask the young fellow in French? "*Bien sur*," he replies and in we go, stepping after him through the gravel entry to the door that leads into a huge inner courtyard. There women sit peeling hundreds of potatoes. A wonderful smell fills the courtyard. Round tables wait for the dozens of yellow tulips arrangements set on a huge sideboard.

A gentleman appears and greets us. He is *Monsieur* Zebulon. He introduces us to his son, Natan, the boy who allowed us to follow him in. *M.* Zebulon explains that this is the beginning of Natan's Bar Mitzvah weekend, a four day Sephardic celebration, today being the first time he has put on *tefillin*,[1] tomorrow he will lead Shabbat services, Saturday

---

1. *tefillin*: two small black boxes containing Biblical passages fastened to leather straps and worn during morning prayer.

he will give his *dvar Torah*[2] and Sunday will be his party. This is the Sephardic way, he explains. And yes, of course, he says, we may enter the synagogue to have a look around.

We tiptoe across the courtyard and enter through the heavy door. The sanctuary is quiet, the 1500 chairs covered in white linen empty below high vaulted ceilings. Everything is dark, carved wood, the central *bima*, the chairs and benches, the women's balcony railing. High carrara marble columns support the enormous room. At the front of the synagogue is a three-story high *ahron kodesh*,[3] wooden doors carved circles marking the twelve tribes, half hidden by maroon velvet curtains drawn back by gold tassels. A huge gold menorah stands in front of the arc just beneath the eternal light which hangs from the high ceiling.

Engraved to the left of the arc is a gold plaque "*a la mémoire de nos glorieux morts* 1939–45." Twelve names are lit, each with both French and Biblical names—Alitenssi, Moise Miche; Aboressi, Isaac Jacques; the Biblical name preceding the French name. These are the war heroes who died in battle. And to the right, the memorial plaque to "*nos soeurs et nos frères,*" the deported.

After sitting for a few moments in the silence, we go into the office to give a donation. We speak a moment to the *Consistoire*[4] officials. "Be sure to see the memorial on the courtyard wall," they say, telling us it will soon be redone. We say good-bye to the officials, the women peeling potatoes, and Mr. Zebulon. Natan has disappeared with a friend.

We stand a moment in the courtyard looking at the enormous memorial carved into grey stone on the synagogue's wall protected by the high wrought iron fence. "*A Nos Martyrs—1940–1944.*" So many families deported, each name delicately carved—nineteen Torres, the Privys a long list also. In total, 1279 Jewish persons were rounded up in Bordeaux and murdered at Auschwitz. Their names glisten in the sun.

Beneath the names of the victims is carved, "This synagogue was profaned by Nazi barbarism." And there is a quote from the Biblical prophet, Malachi "And this have ye done again, covering the altar of the Lord with tears, with weeping and crying out."

It took the survivors and the Jewish community twelve years to clean, rebuild, restore and rededicate the synagogue. Today, it stands in its quiet beauty. And we have been allowed in. Today, unlike so many of the Jews of Bordeaux during the war, we have had a bit of luck: the greeting by young Natan Zebulon and his father; seeing the preparations for another joyous bar mitzvah; and being given the opportunity to spend time in this beautiful, restored synagogue. We say a *shehechiyanu* for this moment and meeting this young man who will carry on the future of the Jewish people of Bordeaux.

---

2.   *dvar Torah*: a talk on the week's Torah portion.
3.   *ahron kodesh*: Holy ark containing Torah scrolls.
4.   *Consistoire*: organization governing Jewish congregations in France.

When Copenhagen's Great Synagogue Stood Empty

You hear only your own footsteps as you walk the cobblestone paths in the sleepy fishing village of Dragor. Half an hour outside Copenhagen, hollyhocks and roses are in full bloom against brightly painted cottages. The green grass on the low thatched roofs is perfectly groomed. Bicycles rest against garden walls. Rowboats dot the small beach and sailboats rock in the shallows. Out over the hazy sea, you can see the Swedish coastline only a mile across the Oresund strait. The village is peaceful. In October of 1943, it seemed much the same, but it wasn't. Danish Jews were hidden everywhere.

On September 29, in 1943 just prior to Rosh Hashanah of that year, Rabbi Dr. Marcus Melchior of Copenhagen's Great Synagogue stunned his congregants at the daily service by telling them to leave their homes immediately and go into hiding. He warned that, as the Germans were tightening their grip on Denmark, they planned to round-up Danish Jews on Rosh Hashanah evening at 10 pm. German ships and trains were waiting to deport them to Germany.

It had taken days for the heads of the Jewish community to believe that this could happen in Denmark where the Jewish community had been welcome for centuries. Finally a German diplomat warned him that there was no time to lose. Now, the watchword was "*Lech Lecha*"(Hebrew: Go, Leave). Rabbi Melchior urged congregants to get to the seacoast immediately and hide until the Danish resistance could get everyone across the strait to neutral Sweden which had already agreed to accept the Jewish refugees.

And so began one of the greatest *mitzvot* (good deeds) during the darkest days of World War II as the Danish people banded together to help their Jewish population. The head of the Lutheran church hid the Rabbi and his family in his home. Civil servants combed phone books looking for Jewish names, calling to offer help. Ambulance and truck drivers took Jews to small towns along the coast. Money was raised to pay fishermen to transport Jewish friends to safety. Within three weeks, more than 7,000 Jews were safely in Sweden.

During the High Holydays of 1943, the synagogue stood empty, its torahs hidden in Lutheran churches. Most Jews were already in hiding The Gestapo rounded up fewer than 500 of Denmark's almost 8000 Jews. And even most of those 500 would survive Theresienstadt because of the constant pressure by the Danes.

Here in this tiny village of Dragor, hundreds of Danish Jews were hiding in churches, homes of strangers, farms, and sheds, waiting for the signal from the resistance to board the next boat. They went in rowboats, kayaks, and fishing boats hidden among fish, locked in storage crates, their children drugged to quiet them during the rough crossings. Several were lost at sea, but more than 7000 Jews made it to Sweden where they remained for eighteen long months until May, 1945 when the war was over. And once home, they found their gardens, pets, belongings cared for by neighbors, and their homes immaculate, just as they had left them.

No other occupied country in Europe pulled together at great personal risk to save their Jews. Denmark became the only nation to be recognized as "Righteous Among Nations" by *Yad Vashem*. It is good to visit the little village of Dragor and look across to Sweden and remember. On this Rosh Hashanah sixty-five years later, it is good to recall the *mitzvot* of the entire nation of Denmark.

Bibliography

Ariege-Pyrenees: Guide Pratique, Offices de tourisme et Syndicats d'Initiative, Foix, France, 2001.

Auschwitz Poems, The: An Anthology, Adam A. Zych, ed. The Auschwitz-Birkenau State Museum, Oswiecim, Poland, 1999.

Bachrach, Deborah, *The Holocaust Library: The Resistance*, Lucent Books, San Diego, 1998.

Bauer, Yehuda. *The Holocaust in Historical Perspective*, University of Washington Press, 1978.

Bauer, Yehuda. *American Jewry and the Holocaust: The American Jewish Joint Distribution Committee, 1935–45*. Wayne State University Press, MI, 1981.

Baumel, Judith Tydor. *Double Jeopardy: Gender and the Holocaust*, Vallentine Mitchell & Co. Ltd., London. 1998.

Berg, Ruby Rohrlich, ed. *Resisting the Holocaust*, Oxford Press, England, 1998.

Block, Gay and Drucker, Malka. *Rescuers: Portraits of Moral Courage in the Holocaust*, Holmes & Meier Publishers, Inc., New York, NY, 1992.

Brandeis, Friedl Dicker, *Exhibition to Commemorate the 90th Anniversary of her Birthday*, The State Catalogue and History, Jewish Museum in Prague, 1988.

Borowski, Tadeusz. *This Way to the Gas, Ladies and Gentlemen and Other Stories*, Viking Press, NY. 1967

Bowen, Steven. *Jewish Resistance in Wartime Greece*, Valentine Mitchell, London, 2006.

Burns, Michael, Dreyfus: *A Family Affair, 1789–1945*. Harper Collins, New York, 1991.

Campion, Joan. *In the Lion's Mouth: Gisi Fleischmann and the Jewish Fight for Survival*, University Press of American, Lanham, MD 1987.

Cowles, Virginia. *The Rothschilds: A Family of Fortune*, Alfred A. Knopf, New York, 1973.

Daniels, Elaine Makris, ed. *Growing Up Greek in South Bend: The Early Years*, Tegea Press, Bethesda, MD, 2001.

DioGuardi, Shirley Cloyes. "Jewish Survival in Albania & the Ethics of Besa," *Congress Monthly*, American Jewish Congress, New York, NY, January/February, 2006.

Dobroszycki, Lucjan, ed. *The Chronicle of the Lodz Ghetto: 1941–1944*, Yale University Press, New Haven, CT, 1987.

Duda, Eugeniusz. *Jewish Cracow: A Guide to the Jewish Historical Buildings and Monuments of Cracow*, Vis-à-vis/Etiuda Publishers, Crakow, 2003.

Eibeshitz, Anna and Jehoshua, eds. *Women in the Holocaust*, Volume 1, Remember, Brooklyn, NY 1993.

Ehrenberg, Ilya and Grossman, Vasily, eds. *The Black Book*, Yad Vashem, Holocaust Library, New York, 1980.

Encyclopedia of the Holocaust, MacMillan Publishing Co., New York, 1990.

Feingold, Henry L. *Bearing Witness: How America and Its Jews Responded to the Holocaust*, Syracuse University Press, 1995.

Friedenson, Joseph and Kransler, David. *Heroine of Rescue: The Incredible Story of Recha Sternbuch who Saved Thousands from the Holocaust*. Mesorah Publications, ltd. Brooklyn, NY, 1984.

Geier, Arnold. *Heroes of the Holocaust*, Londonbooks, Miami, FL, 1993.

Gabitz, Gerard. *Les Déportations de Refugies de Zone Libre en 1942*. l'Harmatton, Paris, 1988.

Gardiner, Muriel. *Code Name "Mary": Memoires of an American Woman in the Austrian Underground*, Yale University Press, New Haven and London, 1983.

Gershman, Norman. *Besa: Muslims Who Saved Jews in WW II*, Syracuse University Press, Syracuse, NY, 2008.

Gilbert, Martin. *Atlas of the Holocaust*, William Morrow & Co., New York, NY, 1993.

Goubet, Michel and Debauges, Paul. *Histoire de la Resistance dans la Haute-Garonne*, Editions Milan, 1986.

Grossman, Vasily and Ehrenberg, Ilya. *Dos Shvartsebukh (The Black Book)*, Yad Vashem, Jerusalem, 1984.

Gurewitsch, Brana, ed. *Mothers, Sisters, Resisters: Oral Histories of Women Who Survived the Holocaust*, University of Alabama Press, Tuscaloosa, 1998.

Halter, Marek. *Stories of Deliverance: Speaking with Men and Women who rescued Jews from the Holocaust*, Open Court, Chicago, IL, 1998.

Hart, Janet. *New Voices in The Nation: Women and the Greek Resistance, 1941–1964*, Cornell University Press, Ithaca, NY, 1996.

Heinemann, Marlene E., *Gender and Destiny: Women Writers and the Holocaust*, Greenwood Press, New York, 1986.

Hewett, Nelly Trocme, Interview at her home, St. Paul, MD, June 30, 2001.

Holloway, Marguerite. "Profile: Rita Levi-Montalcini," *Scientific American*, January, 1993

Holocaust Chronicle: A History in Words and Pictures, Publications International, Ltd., Lincolnwood, IL, 2000.

Iranek-Osmecki, Kasimiera. *He Who Saves One Life*, Crown Publishing Co., New York. 1971.

Jancar-Webster, Barbara. *Women and Revolution in Yugoslavia 1941–1945*. Arden Press, Inc., Denver, CO, 1990

Kakis, Frederic. *Legacy of Courage: A Holocaust Survival Story in Greece*, First Books, Bloomington, IN, 2003.

Kapralski, Slawomir, ed. *The Jews in Poloand: Volume II*. Judaica Foundation, Center for Jewish Culture, Cracow, Poland, 1999.

Kladstrup, Donald and Petie Kladstrup, *Wine and War: The French, the Nazis, and the Battle for France's Greatest Treasure*, Broadway Books, New York, NY, 2001.

Koestler, Arthur. *Scum of the Earth*, The Macmillan Co., New York, 1941 (original publication by Cape, Great Britain).

La Depeche du Midi (newspaper of Toulouse, Fr.), "Regine," July 22, 1941.

Laska, Vera, ed. *Women in the Resistance and in the Holocaust: The Voices of Eyewitnesses*, Greenwood Press, Westport, CT. 1983

Lazar, Lucien. *Rescue as Resistance: How Jewish Organizations Fought the Holocaust in France,* Columbia University Press, NY. 1996.

Levi-Montalcini, Rita. *In Praise of Imperfection: My Life and Work*. Basic Books, Inc. New York. 1988.

Lixl-Purcell, Andreas, ed. *Women of Exile: German-Jewish Autobiographies Since 1933*, Greenwood Press, New York, NY, 1988.

Lottman, Herbert R. *The French Rothschilds*, Crown Publishers, Inc, New York, 1995.

Lusting, Arnost. *A Prayer for Katarina Horovitzova*, Interlink Publishing Group, Northampton, MA, 1990.

Malkin, Peter Z. & Stein, *Harry. Eichmann in my Hands*, Warner Books, New York, NY, 1990

Marble, Alice (with Dale Leatherman). *Courting Danger: My Adventures in World-Class Tennis*, Golden-Age Hollywood, and High-Stakes Spying, St. Martin's Press, NY, 1991.

Margosis, Michel. Testimony and interview, U.S. Memorial Holocaust Museum, March 14, 2001.

Matsas, Michael. *The Illusion of Safety: The Story of the Greek Jews During the Second World War*, Pella Publishing Co., New York, NY, 1997.

Muus, Flemming B. and Varinka Wichfeld. *Monica Wichfeld: A Very Gallant Woman*, Arco Publishers, Ltd. London, 1955.

Neumann, Johanna Jutta (Gerechter). *Via Albania: A Personal Account*, Silver Spring, Md, 1990.

Niewyk, Donald & Nicosia, Francis. *The Columbia Guide to the Holocaust*, Columbia University Press, NY, 2000.

Norges Hjemmefrontmuseum: Norway's Resistance Museum, Trykk: Centraltrykkeriet Grafisk Service AS, 1982.

Nossiter, Adam. *The Algeria Hotel: France, Memory and the Second World War*, Houghton Mifflin Company, New York, NY. 2001

Ofer, Dalia and Weitzman, Lenore J., eds. *Women in the Holocaust*, Yale University Press, New Haven, 1998.

Paldiel, Mordecai. *Sheltering the Jews: Stories of Holocaust Rescuers*, Fortress Press, Minneapolis, 1996.

Paldiel, Mordecai. *The Path of the Righteous: Gentile Rescuers of Jews During the Holocaust*, KTAV Publishing House, Inc., in association with The Jewish Foundation for Christian Rescuers/ADL , New York, 1993.

Paxton, Robert O. *Vichy France: Old Guard and New Order 1940–1944*, Knopf, New York, NY, 2001 (second edition).

Petrow, Richard, *The Bitter Years: The Invasion and Occupation of Denmark and Norway April 1940–May 1945*, William Morrow & Co., New York, NY, 1974.

Porter, Darwin and Danforth Prince, *Frommer's Norway*, Third Edition, Wiley Publishing, Inc., Hoboken, NJ, 2007.

Porter, Jack Nusan, ed. *Jewish Partisans: A Documentary of Jewish Resistance in the Soviet Union During WW II, Vol 1*, University Press of America, Lanham, MD. 1982.

"Profile: Rita Levi-Montalcini," *Scientific American*, January, 1993 (pp 12–13)

Pundik, Herbert. *In Denmark It Could Not Happen: The Flight of the Jews to Sweden in 1945*, Gefen Publishing House, Jerusalem, Israel, 1998.

Ramet, Sabrina, ed. *Gender Politics in the Western Balkans: Women and Society in Yugoslavia and the Yugoslav Successor States*. Penn State University Press, University Park, PA, 1999.

Rebiger, Bill. *Jewish Sites in Berlin* (Third Revised Edition). Jaron Verlag GmbH, Berlin, Germany, 2003.

Reilly, Robin, *The Sixth Floor: The Danish Resistance Movement and the RAF Raid on Gestapo Headquarters*, March, 1945, Cassell & CO., London, UK, 1969, 2002.

Ringelblum, Emanuel. *Notes From the Warsaw Ghetto*, translated by Jacob Sloan, McGraw Hill, New York, 1958.

Rittner, Carol and Roth, John. *Different Voices: Women and the Holocaust*, Paragon Press, New York. 1993.

Ritvo, Roger A. and Plotkin, Diane M., *Sisters in Sorrow: Voices of Care in the Holocaust*, Texas A&M University Press, College Station, TX, 1998.

Roth, Chaya H. *The Fate of Holocaust Memories: Transmission and Family Dialogues*, Palgrave, Macmillan, New York, NY, 2008.

Rothschild, Guy de. *The Whims of Fortune: The Memoirs of Guy de Rothschild*, Random House, New York, NY, 1985 (translation copyright).

Rubin, Susan Goldman. *Fireflies in the Dark: The Story of Friedl Dicker-Brandeis and the Children of Terezin*, Holiday House, NY, 2000.

Sarner, Harvey. *Rescue in Albania: One Hundred Percent of Jews in Albania Rescued from Holocaust*, Brunswick Press, Cathedral City, CA, 1997.

Schindler, Emilie {with Erika Rosenberg}. *Where Light and Shadow Meet: A Memoir*, W.W. Norton, NY, 1996.

Sliwowska, Wiktoria (translated from Polish by Julian and Fay Bussgang). *The Last Eyewitnesses: Children of the Holocaust Speak*, Northwestern University Press, Evanston, IL, English translation copyright, 1998.

Stadtler, Bea. "Jewish Women in Holocaust Resistance," in *Holocaust Literature: A Handbook of Critical, Historical and Literary Writings*, Saul S. Friedman, ed. Greenwood Press, Westport, CT. 1993.

Street, Brian Jeffrey. *The Parachute Ward: A Canadian Surgeon's Wartime Adventures in Yugoslavia*, Editio Online Publishing, ltd, 1987, 1998.

Sutherland, Christine. *Monica*, Farrar, Straus, & Giroux, New York, NY, 1990.

Ten Boom, Corrie (with John and Elizabeth Sherril). *The Hiding Place*, Bantam Books, NY, 1971.

Tomazzewski, Irene and Werbowski, Tecia. *The Rescue of the Jews in Poland*, Price Patterson, Ltd. Montreal. 1994.

Top 10 Copenhagen (Eyewitness Travel Guide), DK Publishing, New York, NY, 2007.

Unger, Michal, "The Status and Plight of Women in the Lodz Ghetto," *Women in the Holocaust*, Yale U. Press, New Haven, 1998.

Valley, Eli. *The Great Cities of Central and Eastern Europe*, Rowman & Littlefield Publishers, Lanham, MD, 2005.

Weitz, Margaret Collins. *Sisters in the Resistance*, John Wiley & Sons, Inc. New York, 1995.

Women Surviving the Holocaust: Proceedings of the Conference, Institute for Research in History. Esther Katz and Joan Miriam Ringelheim, eds. New York, 1983.

Zucotti, Susan. *The Holocaust, The French, and the Jews*. Basic Books, New York, NY. 1993.

Zucotti, Susan. *The Italians and the Holocaust: Persecution, Rescue, and Survival*. Basic Books, Inc. New York, 1987.

Zych, Adam A., ed., *The Auschwitz Poems: An Anthology*, Auschwitz-Birkenau State Museum, Osweicim, Poland, 1999.

Interviews

Johanna Jutta Neumann, survivor whose family was hidden in various homes in Albania during the War, Silver Spring, MD, 2010.

Stella Levi, survivor of Rhodes round-up and deportation to Auschwitz. Rhodes, Greece, July, 2005.

Perla Brandriss, who was hidden in a home for tubercular children in Lille, France. Silver Spring, MD, many conversations between 1996 and present.

Nelly Trocme Hewett, daughter of Magda Trocme, St. Paul, Minnesota, June 30, 2001.

Michel Margosis, son of Schendel Margosis, April 11, April 21, October 18, 2001.

Anna Nesparova, Lidice Survivor, Lidice, Czech Republic, September 24, 2000.

Helen Ostrow, rescued by Baroness Rothschild, now resides in Cincinnati, October 23, 2001.

Teresa Swiebocka, Editor of the Auschwitz-Birkenau State Museum, Oswiecim, Poland, September 21, 2000.

A Note on the Author

B orn and raised in Texas and Oklahoma, Davi Walders graduated from the University of Texas at Austin. Since then, she has made her home in the Washington, DC area where she received an M.A. in Linguistics from The American University and continued graduate work in Human Development at the University of MD, College Park.

She is a writer and educator whose poetry and prose have appeared in more than 200 publications, including *The American Scholar, JAMA, Feminist Studies, Lilith*, and *Potomac Review*. Her work is included in such anthologies as *Worlds in Their Words: Contemporary American Women Writers* (Prentice Hall); *Literature of Spirituality* (MMM Publishing), *Beyond Lament: Poets of the World Bearing Witness to the Holocaust* (Northwestern University Press), Lonely Planet's *Tales from Nowhere*, and *Traveler's Tales: Prague*.

Her chapbook, *Gifts: Poem Portraits of Gifted Individuals Who Valued Giving*, was commissioned by the Milton Murray Foundation for Philanthropy and presented by the Carnegie Corporation to its Carnegie Medal of Philanthropy recipients. She received the Greater Washington Hadassah's Myrtle Wreath Award for developing and directing the Vital Signs Poetry Project at the National Institutes of Health and its Children's Inn in Bethesda, MD, which was funded for three years by The Witter Bynner Foundation for Poetry. She edited the Project's *Using Poetry in Therapeutic Settings: A Resource Manual & Poetry Collection*.

Her numerous awards include an Artist Grant in Poetry from the Maryland State Arts Council; a National Endowment for the Humanities Summer Fellowship; a Puffin Foundation grant; an Alden B. Dow Creativity Fellowship; a Time Out for Women Grant from the ARIL, the Association for Religion and Intellectual Life; a President's Grant from Montgomery County, MD Arts and Humanities Council; and residencies at Blue Mountain Center, Ragdale Foundation, and Virginia Center for the Creative Arts. Her work has been read by Garrison Keillor on Writer's Almanac, performed in New York City and elsewhere, and nominated for Pushcart Prizes.

When Davi is not writing, teaching, or giving readings, she enjoys traveling with her husband and spending time with her daughters and five grandsons.

"To champion the orphaned,
the oppressed
that mortals of the earth
tyrannize no more"
(Psalm 10:18)